THOSE WERE THE DAYS

A compilation of local artistes in an entertainment revue
of Carlisle & district 1950-1970

Marie K Dickens & Geoff Dickens

HAYLOFT

First published 2004

Hayloft Publishing, Kirkby Stephen,
Cumbria, CA17 4DJ

tel: (017683) 42300
fax. (017683) 41568
e-mail: dawn@hayloft.org.uk
web: www.hayloft.org.uk

ISBN 1 904524 12 5

A catalogue record for this book is available
from the British Library

Produced in Great Britain
Printed and bound in Hungary

Those were the days is dedicated to the audience

ACKNOWLEDGMENTS

FIRSTLY we would like to say a very big thank you to everyone featured in *Those Were the Days* who have provided us with personal information, memories and photographs. We would also like to thank Cumbrian Newspapers for permission to reproduce information and the many photographs which originally appeared in the local newspapers of the times. A big thank you to the staff of Cumbria Heritage Services, Carlisle Castle. Also to Stephen White, Alec Alves and the staff of Carlisle Library for their help and local historian Denis Perriam. We must also say a big thank you to Kathleen Dickens for the compilation of the A to Z list of entertainers and proof reading. Thank you also to the following for sharing their personal memories and Photographs with us.

Carol Sterling, grand daughter of Ronnie Atkinson.
Isobel Irving, photographer of the 1950s/60 s.
Liz Stephenson, daughter of Bill Stephenson
Tom Lomas, for memories and photographs of Dave Batey and the BATS.
Pete Hoban, for memories and photographs of Cliff Eland and the BATS.
Christian Dymond of *Cumbria Life*, for memories of the Cliff Eland Big Band.
Mr & Mrs John Minns of Silloth, for pre-War Dance Hall and Cinema memories.
Claire Thomas, daughter of Mick Potts.
Joy Irving, daughter of Rita Irving.
Gordon Halliwell for what is probably the only surviving photograph to include Lance Armstrong.
Brian and Sandra Codona.
Moyra Purves and Heather Cowperthwaite, wife and daughter of the late Ray Purves.
My aunt, Norah Reid, for her memories of my uncle Roland and the Abbey Singers.
Nora Kenyon, wife of the late Frank Kenyon.
Mr Derek Parker for his memories of the Edenaires.

CONTENTS

INTRODUCTION

Many of the earlier bands and their members mentioned here had been on the scene during the 1930s and 1940s, so why single out the 1950s and 60s you may ask? Well, because my parents and those of you approaching retirement age and older can often be heard saying: 'Ah, those were the days' when referring to these years.

My father, Geoff Dickens, who himself was and still is a local entertainer has recounted to me stories of how, many of his friends and acquaintances were big name stars back in the 50s and 60s. While reading through old newspapers at the archives in Carlisle Castle I came across many familiar names and saw for myself that these were not just stories but were based on fact. I found out that many of his friends had truly lived the rock star life, packing out venues locally and further afield, with screaming crowds of fans and many also having fan clubs.

I decided that a book about these stars of yesteryear, and indeed stars of today, for many are still entertaining audiences would be a nostalgic trip down memory lane for those who can recall them, and for future generations to learn that many musically talented people had their roots here in the city. When I began putting the book together I thought who better to team up with than my father, Geoff Dickens, whose own musical career was influenced by the scene and the lads from those days.

Here we have endeavoured to give an insight into the way we were entertained in 50s and 60s by compiling a brief history of Her Majesty's Theatre. Also included are the local venues, the bands that enter-tained there, the local cinemas and the Lonsdale where many famous acts of the era would perform, and the Argyll, which then became the famous Cosmo.

We have attempted to include as many local entertainers and their associates of the 50s/60s scene as possible, including, wherever possible, personal interviews and for those who have left the area or are sadly no longer with us we have collected memories and photographs from their families and friends. Some areas briefly touch on the scene of the early 1970s, here you will notice what a difference a decade can make. For some, gone are their suave suits and short haircuts and in comes the 'hairy' look, Alf Finlayson and Greg 'Alf' Ridley spring to mind. For the many who are still entertaining us today you will find potted histories of their careers from the 1950s/60s to date.

You will note that where we have named bands and their members the same names may appear again with other bands, this is because most of the musicians in the area were friends and associates, so during their careers it was natural that they would perform together or give support to each other. We have endeavoured to show the interface between all the musicians which can clearly be seen throughout the pages of this book, with many not only receiving support and encouragement but in some cases tuition from each other.

We have also included an A to Z list in respect of all those who entertained audiences, some of whom we have not been able to contact prior to publication but their names are remembered here in print.

THE ENTERTAINMENT SCENE OF THE 1950S-1960S

Before taking a look at the local scene I feel it is necessary to take a brief look at what was happening in America at this time, as we were heavily influenced by the Americans. Over in the States the early 1950s began to see the decline in popularity of the singer backed by the big band, about the only thing rising in popularity at the time being the sounds of progressive jazz. From 1951 to the end of 1955 Rock 'n' Roll evolved more or less spontaneously in five parallel styles. Firstly that of the Country Boogie show bands who played a repertoire of Country and Western ranging from Western Swing, Hollywood Cowboy songs, to ballads and dance tunes, with the likes of Bill Hayley being popular at this time.

Then there was the Rhythm and Blues material played by people like Pat Boone. 1954 saw Elvis Presley and the sound of Country rock, otherwise known as Rockabilly - basically a white version of Boogie Blues. The black equivalent to Rockabilly was the Rocking Chicago Blues in the style of Chuck Berry and Bo Diddley. Also there were the sounds of the vocal Rock and Roll groups.

The 1960s saw the piano and saxophone gradually dropped in favour of guitars. At the same time the States saw the rise in popularity of Folk Rock which was eventually renamed simply Rock. Mowtown reached the peak of its popularity in the US charts in the 70s. However that is another story in itself.

Here in Britain by 1950 the war had been over for five years but post war euphoria was still alive, everyone was optimistic about the future. We were listening to BBC radio shows such as *Educating Archie* and *The Clithero Kid*. In the early 1950s we were increasingly influenced by Elvis, Buddy Holly and other trends from the USA; cinema and dance halls were never more popular.

The 1950s saw popular music begin its transition into pop. In 1950 the crooner backed by a big band and the lavishly costumed stage musical still reigned supreme. By the end of the decade they had lost their young audience to their new rivals - Rock 'n' Roll, Trad Jazz, and, in Britain, Skiffle.

In 1950 Carlisle and district entertainment was just beginning to flourish. The growth of industry brought more work and the war years became a distant memory. Carlisle boasted Her Majesty's Theatre, a large number of working men's clubs, youth clubs, village halls, cinemas and dance halls such as the Gretna, the Market Hall, Bonds in the Richmond Hall, the Crown & Mitre, the County Ballroom, the Queen's Hall, the Silver Grill and the Cameo to men-

tion a few. The entertainment at this time was provided by the sound of the big bands, such as the Cliff Eland Band, the Skyliners, the Mayfair Orchestra, the Cyril Lowes Orchestra, the legendary Alf Adamson Orchestra, the Edenaires, who were very popular over the Border, and many more.

It was not until the 1960s that guitar based bands such as the Tornadoes, the Dolls, (later to become the Voltaires), the VIPs, the Danubes, the Hotrods, the Four Dollars, Rue & the Rockets, the Nomads, the Dakotas, the Cave Dwellers (who in 1964 were credited with being 'the birth of the Border Sound') to name but a few, became more popular with youngsters, who by now were also enjoying nights out at Carlisle's first night club, the 101 and Sunday nights entertainment at the Cosmo, in fact they were enjoying entertainment almost every night of the week.

Carlisle's night spots of the 60s (and 70s) played host to not only local talent but many who went on to become big names in the industry - such as Cliff Richard, the Beatles, Helen Shapiro, the Rolling Stones, the Who, the Walker Brothers, the Troggs, Gerry and the Pacemakers, Roy Orbison, the Moody Blues, Jethro Tull, Gene Pitney, Billy Fury, Pink Floyd and many, many more.

It is also interesting to note here, in today's era of manufactured pop stars, a comment featured in the *Carlisle Journal* of July 1966. A teenage popster asked the question, 'What has happened to the beat scene?' The reply, 'It has been demolished by commercialism. Groups are blown up sky high by publicity and people are judging by this rather than the music that is being played.'

The pub scene being slower to start mainly due to the restrictions imposed by state management, but with local dance bands, brass bands, jazz bands and individual performers both singers and comedians, Carlisle's entertainment scene was on the move. The Carlisle and District State Management Scheme of 1921 had its origins as the Liquor Control Board, which was introduced during World War I due to Lloyd George's concern that Carlisle was being affected by the heavy drinking and rowdiness of thousands of workers drafted in to build and work for the massive munitions depot at Gretna. As a result licensing hours were restricted and various rules introduced, for example it became illegal to advertise alcohol and to buy drinks for friends - the 'no treating' rule. The dance venue we all knew as the 'Gretna' on Lowther Street was originally the post office building which was rapidly adapted and reopened on 12 July 1916 as an establishment to meet the needs of these men working at Gretna and living in Carlisle.

The Carlisle and District State Management Scheme became known as the 'Carlisle Experiment' and controlled licensed premises until 1971. It is covered extensively in John Hunt's book *A City Under the Influence*. The Carlisle and District State Management scheme's answer to the introduction of the breathalyser in 1967 which sounded the death knell for the country pub scene was the building of pubs such as the Border Terrier, Morton, at which Sunday nights became the place to be.

1967 also saw the formation of the Border Artistes Theatrical Society, formed for charitable purposes. The BATS continued to entertain at functions through the 70s until their demise in 1982.

Bill Cain, the square dance caller, in action with the Alf Adamson and the the Border Square Dance Band. The band's music was broadcast on the BBC's Barn Dance programme. Photo courtesy of the Carlisle Journal.

HOME ENTERTAINMENT

Geoff recalls at nights people would listen to the radio. I can remember programmes such as *Journey into Space*, *Hancock's Half Hour*, *Dick Barton Special Agent*, *Carol Louis Discoveries with Bobby Laing*, who also appeared at Her Majesty's, *Tales of the Black Museum*, the *Goon Show* and later Radio Luxemburg. The radio was vital on Saturday afternoons for the football results - no one was allowed to make a sound. Popular BBC radio programmes of the early 1950s were the broadcasts of local old time dances and barn dances taking place around the area.

Photographs above and below taken at the Holme Head Works canteen where Miss Florence Wilkinson's troupe gave a display of square dancing. Afterwards the whole company joined in. The Alf Adamson Border Square Dance Band often played at such venues and was broadcast by BBC Radio. Courtesy of the Carlisle Journal February 1952.

New Technology of the 50s & 60s

Left a Decca Capri record player, costing 18 guineas (£18.90p). Middle left, the 1964 way to listen to music. Advertisements from the Carlisle Journal. Lightweight record players could transform a school hall into a dance hall, or bring the stars to your own room.

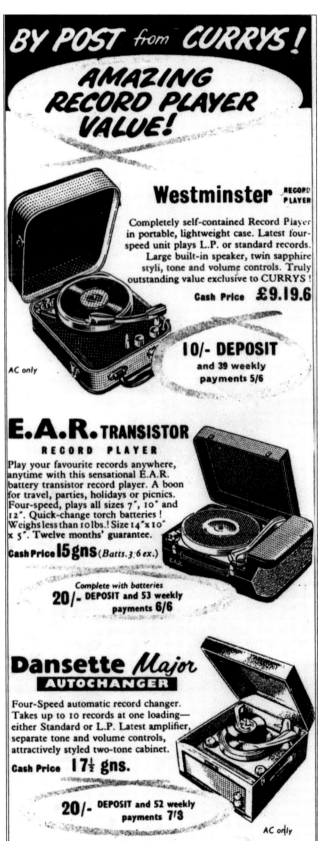

Television

TELEVISION began in the 1930s but it was not until 1950 that the first television pictures were received in the north of the country, even then reception was very poor. Border Television did not start broadcasting until 1960.

Geoff recalls that until a television set arrived at 33 Buchannan road I was often invited into the homes of friends who had this magical item. Gordon Haliwell (bass guitarist later mentioned in this book) would invite me to watch programmes such as *Amos and Andy* and *I Love Lucy*. Another entertainer who lived in the area, who also beat me in the 'I've got a TV race' was Alf Ridley of VIPs' fame.

I would visit cousins on Sunday nights to watch the old gangster movies. Eventually after what seemed like ages I arrived home to see a television aerial had been erected on our roof - television had arrived at number 33 at last.

The television set had now replaced the fireplace as the focal point of the living room, with everyone wanting to own a television to watch the Queen's Coronation in 1952. However not everyone was as pleased as Geoff and his friends were about this magical new invention. The Revd Philip Canham of the church of St Herbert, Carlisle, regarded television as a menace saying, 'Apart from the dubiousness of some of its programmes, this passive form of entertainment involves the wrong use of leisure time.'

Pictures, clockwise from top:
Pictured in the Carlisle Journal in October 1950 - the first TV in the city.
The 1960 look - the new slim-line TV.
Border TV's first presenters, John Cargill, Mary Marquis and Michael Cooper.
Border TV goes on air for the first time on 1 September 1960. Photographs courtesy of the Carlisle Journal.

Her Majesty's Theatre, June 1953,
photograph courtesy of Carlisle Library

The Victoria Hall, built in 1874, became Her Majesty's Theatre and Opera House in the summer of 1879. The theatre suffered a serious fire on 12 September 1904, which curtailed the cinematograph which had appeared in shows from 1897. The interior was rebuilt and re-opened 12 months later with film screenings continuing on an occasional basis.
The theatre was later taken over by Sidney Bacon, the showman. Sidney Bacon Pictures Ltd was well known for Cine Variety Halls in the north. Little is heard of films being shown at Her Majesty's after 1919, with live entertainment proving more popular and profitable.

From then until its closure in 1932 it suffered from fluctuating fortune. The theatre was opened once again on 1 October 1934. In 1936, Silloth born Mr A C Aster bought Her Majesty's and really put the city on the entertainment map.

The fire of 1904, courtesy of Carlisle Evening News.

Mr A C Aster, who died in March 1966.
Picture courtesy of the Carlisle Journal.

Her Majesty's saw many famous actors and operatic stars during its history such as Charlie Chaplin, Buffalo Bill, Sybil Thorndyke, Harry Lauder, Noel Coward, Laurel & Hardy and the Saddlers Wells. It provided entertainment to suit a broad spectrum of theatre going public, with variety shows, musical comedies, pantomimes and circus entertainment. This format proved successful until the mid 1950s when some of the shows flopped and the building began to deteriorate.

The Theatre found it difficult enough to compete with the cinemas but with the boom in television the end was in sight for the theatre and in 1960 Carlisle City Council took a three year lease on it and in 1962 a youth club was opened called the Room at the Top which proved popular with the youth of the day. However in general support from the public was just not there. The final curtain came down in January 1963. The building was later used as a bingo hall and was eventually bought by Daniel Johnstone's, a carpet and furniture firm, which demolished it in 1979 and used the site as a car park, which it still is today.

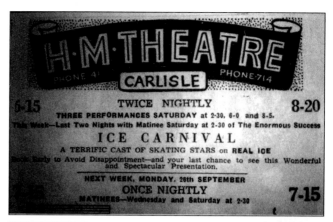

Pictured clockwise from top:

An advertisement for the theatre from 1949
Mr John Sullivan, (left) manager of Her Majesty's, welcoming Mr Harry Neil on his arrival at the theatre for the opening of 'Sunshine Serenade' the resident summer show of 1949.
Pantomime comedians Billy Stutt and Arty Mayne chatting in their dressing room. Carlisle Journal, January 1950.
Maureen Grace, who took part in an Ice Carnival at the Theatre. Carlisle Journal.
Lofty, the 9 ft 3 inch Dutch giant who appeared at Her Majesty's Theatre, Carlisle Journal, March 1948.

Some of the entertainers who appeared at Her Majesty's Theatre

Pictured clockwise from top left,

Ida Ratcliffe (née Thompson), who appeared at the theatre in December 1950. Ida came from Sheffield Street, Carlisle.

Jumbo, the 50-year-old, five-ton elephant with a star's temperament, went on strike when she refused to climb a ramp into Her Majesty's Theatre after she heard it creak. Carlisle Journal, 8 February 1957.

Bobby Laing, winner of many talent contests, and vocalist with Carlisle's Mayfayre Orchestra who sang at H M Theatre. Carlisle Journal, 23 July, 1957.

As the curtains closed for the last time at H M Theatre, comedian Billy Stuff receives gifts from the audience. Carlisle Journal, January 1963.

Pictured clockwise from top:

The cast of a Scottish entertainment at H Majesty's Theatre.

The Four Knights seen hear rehearsing for a fund raising concert in 1959, left to right, Dai Walters, Frank Logan, David Taylor and Herbert Vickers. Carlisle Journal.

The 'Room at the Top' youth club were down in the dumps with the closure of Her Majesty's and had to find an alternative venue in January 1963. The committee, pictured here, are Carole Hutchinson, Penny Kelly, J L Irving, Penny Burch, Susan Carr, Jeff Lawson, Ken Wood and John Roberts.

Stage hands get to work stripping the backstage of pantomime scenery, Carlisle Journal, January 1963.

A wreath on the door of the theatre is a final tribute, paid by former professional actor, Mr Elliott Williams. An inscription read: 'In fond memory - killed by bingo, television and the indifference of the public.' Carlisle Journal, January 1963.

H M Theatre, Lowther Street, became a bingo hall and the first night, 27 September 1963, was a great success with a top prize of a mini car.

Let's Dance

Above, the Jive endurance competition held at Penrith in 1960 takes its toll!

Below jiving at the Cameo, 1961 and some of the men who chose to sit out a dance at the Cameo.

Pictures from a Jive 'endurance' competition held at Penrith in 1960. Pictured above Christine Labram and Malcolm Dixon, and below Sheila Labram and Trevor Brogden.

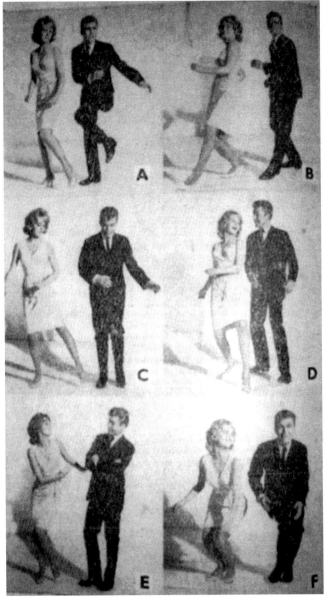

From top, clockwise, the latest dance craze from America - the Twist. Instructions printed in the Carlisle Journal, 1962.

Two of the best Twisters dance to the Basin Street Jazz Boys at a 1962 competition at the Gretna Hall.

Rita Irving dancers in a twist competition

Twisting in the afternoon at the County Ballroom, 1962.

January 1962, the Carlisle Journal gives more instructions for the Twist - 'Turn the foot in one direction, hips in another direction, knees forward, shoulders back - and if you're still standing you're well on the way. All you need to do now is shake! Giving a dance demonstration - Jill Simcox and John Dane. The craze did not last long as in October 1962 the new dance was the Locomotion.

POPULAR VENUES OF THE ERA

The Gretna Tavern, Lowther Street

The Gretna Tavern opened on 12 July 1912. In the early 1960s James Henshaw, father of Jimmy of the VIPs, and Gordon Henshaw of Lemongrass and Country Rovers were licensees of the Gretna. The Gretna was later taken over by Tom Foster who introduced soul nights. These proved to be very popular with their combination of disco and a live soul band. Tom went on to buy the Twisted Wheel, West Walls and turned the Gretna into 'Flopps'.

Jim Henshaw, manager of the Gretna, died at the age of 59, in June 1962. Jim raised a lot of funding for charities, both local and national. Despite being a teetotaller, he did not think it strange that he should be running a tavern.

Two dancers at Carlisle's first Rock 'n Roll session at the Gretna Hall in February 1957.

In March 1965 the Top Hat Club opened in the State-owned Gretna Tavern, despite a foot of snow on the city streets.

In June 1962 the music was hot, really hot. At a teenage rock and twist contest in the Gretna Hall organised by Rita Irving, sparks began to fly. The vocalist was crooning a song called Sixteen Candles when the stage curtains went up in flames. The boys on stage were quick thinking and had the blaze out in seconds and, as soon as the charred curtains were carted off stage, drummer Gordon Hind, nicknamed 'Sparkie', resumed his hot seat and the show went on.

The Queen's Ballroom

This photograph from 1958 shows the former Viaduct Hotel and Queen's Ballroom. The site is now occupied by Tesco's store. Cumberland News.

Rita Irving and her daughter Joy ran local teenage dances, along with Rita's brother Terry. Rita was known as 'a glamourous figure in dancing pumps' and taught children to dance at her Carlisle Dancing School but was equally at home down on the farm.

RITA, JOY & TERRY IRVING'S TEENAGE DANCES
QUEEN'S HALL, FRIDAY, 7.30, 2/6—
    Fantastic Sound of the V.I.P.'s and the BIG 13.
QUEEN'S HALL, SATURDAY, 7.30, 3/——
    By Popular Request, THE BROTHERS GRIM (formerly the Corals) and THE TRIBE.
COUNTY BALLROOM, MONDAY, 7.30, 2/6—
    THE BROTHERS GRIM and ? ? ?
QUEEN'S HALL, SATURDAY MORNING, 10.30, 2/-—
    FABULOUS JUNIOR BEAT CLUB. THE SHADES and BIG 13.

Advertisement for the Irvings' Teenage Dances.

In September 1954 hundreds of soldiers stationed in the area said that their friendships with Carlisle girls are in danger because the Queen's Hall dances have been put out of bounds to them. Resentment was running high at the local camps in Carlisle and Longtown as soldiers were forced to wait outside the dance hall for their girls.

The order was issued from Garrison HQ and was a rebuke to a small element among the servicemen who were banned from the dance hall by the promoter, Mr Tom Fisher. The ban was lifted shortly afterwards and the soldiers were able to dance with their girls again.

The County Ballroom, Botchergate

The County Ballroom, was situated at the top of Botchergate and was part of the County Hotel. The queues for the Saturday night dances would stretch down the flight of stairs, out onto Botchergate and round the corner into the station square, very often stretching as far as the front of the station. At the time the Cyril Lowes Band, as resident band, would provide the main entertainment here, however many other local acts also appeared.

In its early days the County did not sell alcohol. If you wanted a drink you would have your hand stamped to ensure re-admission and would go across to the Red Lion Hotel.

The end of an era came in January 1973 when a major improvement programme began to establish the County and Station Hotel as one of the most luxurious in the area. The 67 bedroom hotel was completely closed for refurbishment and redecoration. The improvements included making a 'Victorianna' restaurant where mood music was played, a residents' lounge, cocktail bar, public bar, men only bar, a lively western theme bar and a 60 seater coffee shop. The famous grand ballroom was transformed into a meeting room to seat up to 80 people and two smaller meeting rooms to hold 12 people. At the time a spokesman for Scottish and Newcastle told the *Cumberland News*, 'We are making the County a 'shop window' for our hotels division.'

The County Hotel, Botchergate, seen here in 1910. Photograph courtesy of Carlisle Library.

In 1949 the County Ballroom was tastefully redecorated and the stage was transferred, in an enlarged form, to the side of the hall, in keeping with a plan often followed in concert and drama halls. The photograph above shows the resident band and their leader, Mr Cyril Lowes, on the new stage.

Below the County Ballroom Band pictured in the early 50s. From left, Cliff Eland and saxophonists Eric Duffell Ralph Pennington and Ken Attwood. Back: piano, John Hogarth; base, Harold Wilkinson; drums, John Corson and trumpet, David Gibson.

Pictured in the Carlisle Journal in October 1954 are competitors in a preliminary round of the national amateur dance competition held in the County Ballroom.

An advertisement for a dance to the Cyril Lowes' Dance Orchestra.

Jock Hymens' Sessionaires, playing at the County, Botchergate, in the early 1960s. The saxophonists are George Pape, baritone; Bob Grice, alto; Sam Bellingham, alto; George Foster, tenor and Bill Finlayson, tenor. The trumpet players are Dickie MacGrath, Jock Hymen and unknown. On the trombones are Don Farley, Cliff Atwood and Mike Crosby and in the rhythm section are Mick Potts, piano; Al Potts, bass and Jimmy Watson, drums. Photograph courtesy of Bill Finlayson.

LOOK! LOOK! LOOK!
WE REGRET THAT THERE WILL BE NO DANCE ON THE FRIDAY OF THIS WEEK OR NEXT WEEK, SO INSTEAD WE ARE MEETING ON WEDNESDAY EVENINGS AT THE

COUNTY BALLROOM

where RODNEY WARR invites you to

SHAKE ★ SHIMMY ★ STOMP

THIS WEEK TO

The Ramrods ★ Rue and the Rockets

plus THE SPINNING TOPS

WEDNESDAY, 13th NOV., 7.30 - 11.30 p.m. ADMISSION 3/-

(Meanwhile of course we continue with the popular Saturday Night Dance)

TOP GROUPS ★ TOP POPS ★ AT THE "COUNTY"

An advertisement from 1963 in the Carlisle Journal.

The Beatles brought the Merseybeat to Carlisle in November 1963 when fans were given souvenir copies of the Evening News by the organisers of a dance at the County Ballroom.

The Crown & Mitre

The Crown & Mitre, pictured in the Carlisle Journal.

Built in 1904, the new hotel replaced the much earlier Crown and Mitre Inn and Coffee House. During the 1950s weekly dances were promoted by Mr Hodgson with music from the Mayfair Dance Band and Bobby Laing. Mr Hodgson received the takings from the door and would pay the band from these and what was left over was his. These dances proved to be so popular, with queues regularly stretching down Castle Street that around 1960 the management of the Crown and Mitre decided to take over the running of dances themselves. Mr Hodgson transferred his custom to the Cosmo, Central Avenue, however regular dances continued at the Crown and Mitre and it is still a popular venue today.

The Mayfair Dance Band played at the Crown & Mitre and are seen here taking part in a competition held at the Cameo, Botchergate, in the late 1940s. From left, back: Boris Sanderson, Bill Stephenson, unknown, Arthur Graham on drums, Jock Hymen and Ted Nixon. Front: George Whitehead, Bob and Dave Ruddick, George Foster and Olly McCauley.

An advertisement for the Mayor's Charity Ball at the Crown & Mitre.

The Carlisle Art's fancy dress ball at the Crown & Mitre, December 1961.

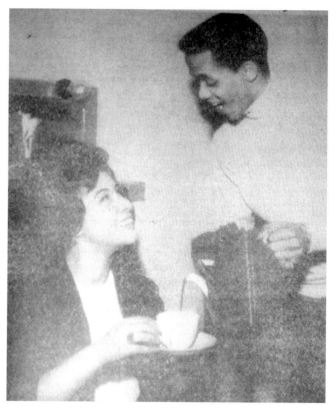

In February 1963 16-year-old Helen Shapiro was appearing at the Lonsdale Cinema and staying at the Crown & Mitre. She and some of the Beatles were invited to a golf club dance by one of the committee members but was soon asked to leave because she wasn't wearing evening dress. Apparently some of the Beatles were wearing leather jackets and a golf club member said, 'It's a private ball, old boy.' Helen said, 'A boy doesn't turn into a hoodlum just because he wears a leather jacket.' Helen is pictured with singer Danny Williams.

The Silver Grill, English Street

The Silver Grill, a licensed restaurant situated on English Street, opened in 1896. It was a popular venue for dinner dances, having the capacity to seat around 300. In 1960 the building under went extensive refurbishment and the restaurant closed in the 70s. The site is now occupied by Boots and W H Smiths.

Pictured above the Cyril Lowes Band in the early 50s, playing in the Pageant Room in the Silver Grill. Back row: Sam Bellingham, vocalist; Dick Jordan, drums; Harold Lowry, piano. Front: possibly Fred Nicholson, trumpet; Ted Barton, Cyril Lowes and George Collins, sax.

Above the Silver Grill, photograph courtesy of the Cumberland News.

Below the Alf Adamson Trio in the Silver Grill, May 1949, at a dinner to celebrate the 150th anniversary of Carlisle firm Hudson Scott & Son Ltd., which by then had become part of the Metal Box Company.

The Ivan Hunter Quintette playing at the Cumberland News social club dinner dance in the Silver Grill in 1952. From left, Arthur Ling, tenor sax; Ivan Hunter, piano; George Baxter, trumpet; Harold Wilkinson, bass and George Mitchellhill, drums.

The Pratchett's dinner dance at the Silver Grill. Seated on the left is Jimmy Stewart, cornet player for St Stephen's Silver Band and father of Elizabeth Stewart.

Pratchett's Engineering dinner dance at the Silver Grill, 1958, (later to become L A Mitchells of Denton Holme),

The Market Hall
(corner of West Tower Street with Market Street)

In September 1952 at a meeting of Carlisle City Council on the letting of the Market Hall for dances, concern was expressed that proper use was not being made of the facilities, which were considered to be the property of the Carlisle ratepayers.

An offer of rent for £1000 had been made by Mr Duncan McKinnon of Melrose for use of the west bay of the Market Hall where he wished to hold dances on Friday and Saturday nights from October 1952 to September 1953. At this, concern was expressed that the council in tying themselves to this deal would not be able to cater for any other events which might crop up. For this reason the Market Hall's committee recommended that the offer should be accepted, whilst at the same time retaining the freedom of use during Coronation week and that the agreement should be on a monthly basis only.

At this time the Market Hall covered a large area with lots of little shops. There was also a concrete floor about the size of three football pitches which would be strewn with white chalk to stop the dancers slipping. It was this area which Duncan, who had turned himself into a company called Border Dances Ltd. planned to turn into the centre of the city's night life. He had taken a long lease from the council, built a stage, cut off the dance hall area from the shops by suspending enormous green tarpaulins, installed many heaters 30 feet up among the iron girders of the roof, and had stuck thousands of little mirrors mounted on cloth around the bottom four feet of the supporting columns.

Duncan McKinnon went on to bring not only local talent in the form of the Edenaires, also known as the Red Coats, but also some big names and acts to the Market Hall. The building became a venue for a variety of entertainment ranging from wrestling, music festivals and regular dances, with live entertainment of both local talent and national entertainers of the era, to exhibitions.

Dance promoter Duncan McKinnon (left) with Carlisle Journal editor Ronald Harrison after judging the 1961 finals of the Teen Personality Contest.

The Alf Adamson Trio music festival in the old Market Hall, 1952, photograph courtesy of Liz Stephenson.

In his book *Owning up* George Melly gives the following description of Duncan McKinnon: "Duncan was an ex-lawyer who lived in Melrose. He was short and plump with an untidy mop of hair, ginger moustache and protuberant eyes. He dressed in wrinkled grey flannels and hairy sports coats with large leather covered buttons. Following his success in running Saturday night hops all over the Borders using local dance bands and small Scottish Groups, he developed larger ambitions, turned himself into a company called Border Dances Ltd. and appointed Jim Godbolt as his London agent... Although several of Duncan's venues were extremely profitable he was always teetering on the edge of disaster because of his obsession with a huge white elephant in the shape of the Market Hall, Carlisle."

Acker Bilk arrived in Carlisle in May 1961 complete with beard and fancy waistcoat but minus the famous bowler hat. Acker said, 'Man, they gave me this crazy tam in Glasgow. I like it. But will it hold as much cider as the bowler?'

An advert from June 1956.

Above Danny Williams at the Market Hall in Carlisle after his hit 'Moon River'. He sang to 300 screaming fans.

Below a queue forms outside the Market Hall to hear Ricky Valance sing in June 1961.

A rapt audience as Ricky Valance sings.

Below the Merseybeats played the Market Hall in December 1963. From left, Aaron Williams, Tony Crane, Billy Kinsley and John Banks.

Above, August 1961 saw a jazz festival at the Market Hall with stars such as Johnny Dankworth, Anita O'Day, Terry Lightfoot and his New Orleans Jazz Band, Bob Wallis and the Storyville Jazz Men, the Original Downtown Syncopaters and Forrie Cairns and his Clansmen.

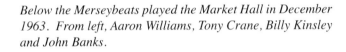

The new Market Assembly Halls, February 1965.

In February 1965 the west bay of the covered market was transformed into the biggest, modern style, emporium between Glasgow and Blackpool. At a cost of £40,000 the new Market Assembly Hall's 10,000 square feet of floor space had a holding capacity of 2,000. It boasted the longest bar in the city and now attracted other events such as big national conferences, banquets, balls and of course the now weekly Border Dances.

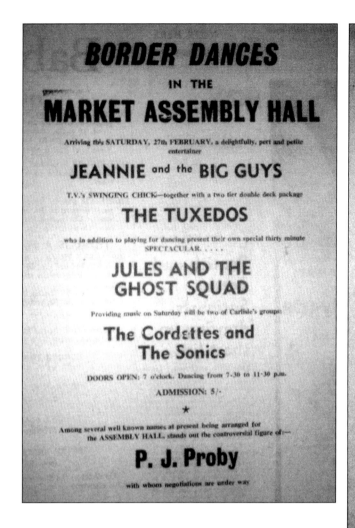

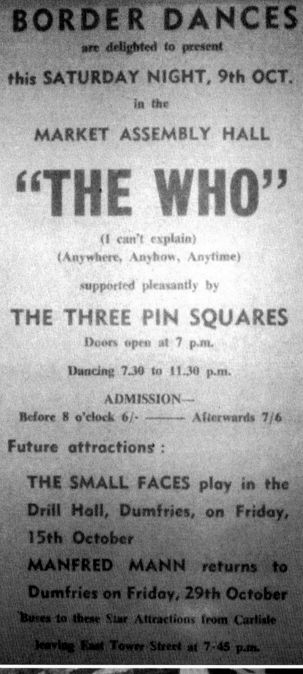

Adverts for events at the Market Assembly Hall, February 1965.

Below a charity fashion show at the Market Assembly Hall, organised by Littlewoods and the Lions Club.

Manfred Mann in Carlisle 1965.

Acker Bilk, playing at Carlisle's Market Hall.

The biggest ever barbecue and kebab event in Carlisle, 1969.

Young competitors at the old-time ballroom dancing competition at Carlisle's Market Hall, November 1968.

An advert for wrestling at the Market Hall, 1968.

Pictured below some of the 1400 crowd at the mammoth barbecue to raise money for the Evening News and Star's appeal for old people and a testimonial fund for Carlisle United's trainer, Dick Young.

John Lee Hooker took part in an American Folk Blues and Gospel festival in Carlisle Market Hall, July 1969.

32

United Services' Club

The board of directors of the United Services' Club soon after its formation in 1950.

In October 1950 Carlisle ex-servicemen achieved a great ambition with the opening of their new club rooms in the old Cecil Hotel on Cecil Street. The first stewards were Mr T.Moore who had 24 years service with the Border Regiment and his wife.

On its closure the Cecil Street Hotel had been taken over by the Royal Navy and the Royal Marines' Association. Although the members put a lot of time and trouble into the venture it was not the success it was hoped it would be. Then came the formation of a central advisory committee of the different ex-service associations and the idea of a joint HQ. The committee received an offer from an anonymous source to purchase the Cecil Hotel premises as a club, which could be rented with an option to buy when they found it financially possible.

The main room downstairs was adapted as a smoking room, with a bar at one end and was decorated in battleship grey, a tribute to its former owners. On the first floor, the main room was converted into a meeting place decorated in sunshine yellow. The three smaller rooms were set aside for card games, reading and committee purposes.

At the time of opening the top floor with its seven rooms was unused. These were eventually developed into entertainment venues. At one time the resident band was the Lance Armstrong Trio who were very popular, with Lance Armstrong playing the organ, Raymond Purvis on drums and Gordon Halliwell on bass guitar. The club also had competing billiards and darts teams.

The United Services' Club chairman Mr F I Mattinson tries out the beer pump watched by Mrs Moore, Mr T Moore and Col. J Richens, one of the board of directors.

The Lance Armstrong Trio with Ray Purves, Lance Armstrong and Gordon Halliwell, also including singer Barry Lytollis on the right. Photograph courtesy of Gordon Halliwell.

The NAAFI Club, Rickergate

Photograph of the NAAFI Club in Rickergate.

The College of Art annex in Rickergate. Behind it is the Civic Centre. Photograph courtesy of the Carlisle Journal, April 1963.

The NAAFI Club was established during the war years to meet the social and entertainment needs of the service men and women based in Carlisle at Hadrians Camp, Houghton and Durranhill Camp, now Rosehill Industrial Park. The NAAFI Club had proved to be popular, but there was never any doubt that the establishment was only to be temporary during the war years.

After the war it became the venue for the Eden Youth Club where, amongst others, local stars such as Maurice Petry and Dave Storey began their careers. The NAAFI was also used as a school dining room at the time. In 1963 it was used as an annex classroom for students of the College of Art.

The NAAFI Club and the adjoining buildings of the Bay Horse Inn and the Fox and Hounds were demolished in the 1960s to make way for development of the Civic Centre. The site of the NAAFI is now the car park on the opposite corner to the Debenhams store.

Demolishing the old NAAFI. Photograph courtesy of Carlisle Journal, September 1966.

The Carlisle Royal Air Force Association's Christmas treat for children at the Eden Youth Centre.

The Green Room Theatre, West Walls

Members of the Fortune Players take time a rest from renovating and decorating their premises in West Walls, April 1954

During the spring of 1954 a transformation took place down in the heart of what was part of the city wall of old Carlisle. A group of enthusiastic drama lovers known as the Fortune Players Green Room Club began renovating and redecorating a newly acquired musty old place at West Walls. The Fortune Players were a part of a larger group, as the Green Room included members from several societies.

Rather than wait for Civic Halls and little theatres to be built the group decided to get on with the construction of their own theatre. They worked to designs by Elfreda Nelson, the wife of the club's director of production, Anthony Nelson. The club consisted of a play-reading room and a sound proof theatre capable of seating around 100 people. In addition the extensive cellars were adapted as workshops for scene painting and for the construction and storage of large props. The Green Room Theatre is still in existence today.

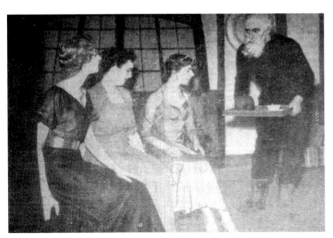

A scene from 'Heartbreak House', a Shaw comedy, performed by the Green Room Club Players at the West Wall Theatre in February 1955. Photograph courtesy of the Carlisle Journal.

In January 1969 a fire swept through the theatre destroying part of the stage and some curtains. The theatre was back in action two months later.

The *Carlisle Journal* printed two articles by Ian Knight in January 1954 about the city's night life. They give a good idea of the type of entertainment on offer.

I made a quick survey of Carlisle dance halls, calling first at the Mitre which is still as popular as ever. Inimitable George Whitehead and the Mayfayre Club Band have been firmly entrenched there for longer than my memory likes to recall.

I was particularly impressed by the line up on an all-saxophone front line - five saxes in all. This type of outfit seems to suite the clientele of the Mitre and I noticed, among a very happy Saturday night crowd, footballers Dennis Stokoe, Tommy Kinlock and Bobby Harrison, looking very fit after their Workington encounter. Also good to see Peter 'Tottle' McGlone still enjoying his dancing.

It was a very pleasant half-hour I spent at the Queens. Promoter Tom Foster deserves hearty congratulations for an intriguing and modern ballroom lighting system he has personally just had installed. The Queens has been most tastefully re-decorated and has a new cosy look. The band, under the leadership of Lawrence Foster, was 'in the groove' and I noticed Nicky Dixon's 'bopping' in the latest American style. (Oh Nicky! Where did you develop your new crew cut?. It seemed to suit his charming partner Margaret, another 'bop' fan.

Evergreen Cyril Lowes still packs 'em in at the County. Good to see Eddie Barton (tenor), Dick Jordan (drums) and Harold Lowry (piano) still holding more than their own with the youngsters. Of course, Cyril has always moved with the times and has a most enthusiastic following of 'bobby soxers'.

On enquiring from the dancers at the County, their most popular tune I was pleasantly surprised to find that way ahead of all others was 'Drag Net' and I was implored on all sides to listen for Cyril's interpretation of this popular number.

Popped in to the Cameo, which was very well attended. The Cameo Band directed by versatile David Ruddick, is extremely popular with the many Cameo fans. Manager Tom Hodgson has just had installed a new amplification system and I am eagerly looking forward to hearing popular vocalist Bobby Laing on this microphone.

The Swimming Club dance in the Mitre last Friday was a very merry affair and Mr and Mrs Charles Galbraith, Mr and Mrs Richard Glaister and Mr and Mrs Ernest Maxwell caught my eye - they appeared to be making up a very jovial party.

Have just heard that Ivan Hunter has formed a new and bigger band and that the line up will be two altos (Ken Atwood and George Pape), tenor (Arthur Ling), trombone (Robert Gordon), bass (Harold Wilkinson), drums (George Mitchell) and, of course, Ivan himself on piano. Now I should think that this outfit will grace many a platform at 'Melody Makers' contests. Ivan tells me he is scoring his own arrangements for the forthcoming contests.

I believe that Scottish promoter Duncan MacKinnon is negotiating with some top class outfits to play some one night stands at the Market Hall. I understand that one of the bands is right out of the top drawer.

In sharp contrast to Dixieland jazz, swing and 'bop', I am delighted to find that in these changing times the old-time dances such as 'Three Drops o' Brandy', the barn dance and the hesitation waltz, can still hold their own as a Saturday night amusement.

Doing very well out of these elegant dances of yester-year are the Carlisle Liberal Association who have been running old-time Saturday night dances for over seven years in the lecture hall of the Viaduct Hotel. The Arcadians Band, who specialise in old time music, have played for this dance since its initiation in June 1946.

What amazed me is that these dancers are very young - either teenagers or in their early twenties. Yet they could, with the greatest dexterity and grace, dance the dances that their mothers and fathers, aye, and their grandmothers and grandfathers danced, before them. This friendly dance has a strong 'country' flavour and I noticed in town for the night were Kathleen, Jean and Gladys Whitfield of Great Orton, Isabella Brown of Orton and Miss Margaret Graham of Stainton.

The Inner Wheel Club held their exclusive dinner

and dance at the Silver Grill. Miss Daphne Telford in a lovely blue floral off-shoulder evening gown did a magnificent job as MC and kept the dance on the move the whole of the evening.

It was interesting to note that lace evening gowns were predominant. Mrs Vaughan Davies, the president of the club, and Mrs R J Hughes, vice-president made excellent speeches and Alderman George Bowman exceeded himself with a most delightful response.

The music for the dancing, which was thoroughly enjoyed by all, was played by Alfred Adamson and his orchestra. Messrs Dias and Co, the large motor firm, also held their annual dance at the Silver Grill.

Youth Clubs of 1955

Local Education Authority Youth Service Clubs at this time included the Botcherby Youth Club, Caldewgate Old boys' Club, Currock Mixed Youth Club, Denton Holme Youth Club, Eden Youth Club, Newtown Youth Club, Petteril Bank Youth Club, Stanwix and Etterby Youth Club and the Upperby Mixed Youth Club.

Pictured below an 'end of session' dance was organised by the Carlisle LEA Youth Clubs at the Cameo Ballroom. Photograph courtesy of the Carlisle Journal.

Kirklinton Hall, The Border Country Club

Kirklinton Hall seen here in the 1940s is situated 10 miles from Carlisle.

The hall had mixed fortunes over the years. It was built of stones from a nearby castle, parts of the building seeming to date from about 1650, but the newer part had been rebuilt in 1875, and it was in turn the seat of the Dacre, Ewart and Kirklinton families. It was also used as a school for a time and then by the RAF during the war years. It was later ran as a 65 roomed hotel, until the 1960s when half of the hall was given over to become the Border Country Club ran by Mr David Hay and his wife. Rumour has it that at one time Kirklinton Hall was also a favourite haunt of notorious gangsters such as the infamous Kray Twins.

In the hotel side, a popular singer/guitarist called Maurice Petry performed most Saturday nights before he took up residency at the Golden Fleece, Ruleholme.

In January 1964 Mr Hay established the county's first casino here with Jane Ramsey as croupier. The roulette and *chemin de fer* tables proved to be so popular that soon after the casino was extended to include Black Jack and Chemmy Dice. The maximum stake on the roulette table was £10. Gambling would go on with coffee and sandwiches laid on until the last punter quit the tables, which were equally available to the housewife having a half-crown flutter and the dedicated gambling man. The club membership grew to around 1600 members, regular cabaret nights were introduced to add to the attractions which already included dancing, wining and dining, and for the celebrator who goes to town a driver was provided to take him home.

March 1964 saw the county's first striptease show take place at the Border Country Club, with Mitzi, 'Britain's pocket Venus' and Tina.

In March 1965 Kirklinton Hall was taken over by Mr Ted Cain. The following October he opened the infamous Regency Ballroom. Ted Cain was a go-ahead character who had some weird and wonderful ways of promoting the club's Regency Ballroom. One of his schemes was the Phantom Arrow, a masked dart player who if you beat him, gave you £10. Other interesting acts were a troupe of Dutch high wire artistes and an act which consisted of performing dogs which ended in disaster with dogs running wildly round the ballroom incensed by the smell of a spilled glass of Pernod.

In 1967 with the introduction of the breathalyser the popularity of the club began to wane so Mr Cain resorted to more strip tease artists, which didn't go down well with the local constable, who closed the club for a few months. In 1969 a High Court ruling on the deeds preceded the winding up of the club leading Ted Cain to return to the south.

After its closure the building became a headache for the police as thieves and vandals moved in and the former stately home became a wreck. It stood forlornly in its extensive grounds, a raided, half ruined shell where birds nested in the wrecked bar fittings and betting tables and where the sound of crumbling plaster had replaced the feet of dancers.

In 1973 the hall was bought by Mr Jim Wainwright, a freelance journalist from London, who had once played the piano there in its hey day as a night club. He had already gained planning permission to convert the property into four large flats. However the property was later badly damaged by fire and has stood in a derelict state since.

Mitzi, the girl in Cumbria's first striptease show.

37

Norman Healey-Creed, jazz man with a difference, playing a razor blade dispenser at the Border Country Club.

Below, the Tiller Girls are pictured after they opened the new Regency Ballroom at the Border Country Club.

THE BORDER COUNTRY CLUB

Look forward to welcoming all members and friends for another Colossal Week-end's Entertainment

CABARET - DANCING - RESTAURANT
ROULETTE
BOTH SATURDAY & SUNDAY EVENINGS

Artistes appearing this Week-end include

KEITH KELLY
(Radio's Wizard of Guitar and Harmonica)

DOROTHY JENNINGS
(Dancing at its Best)

THE FABULOUS

FOUR DOLLARS

MAURICE PETRY serenades in our Restaurant as usual

(Remember no cover charge whatsoever)

P.S.—We still sell
Pints at 1/5.
Atmosphere Free!

Above an advert for an event at the Border Country Club, October 1965.

Below pictures from the Cumberland News in 1973 of vandal-hit Kirklinton Hall.

The Astra Restaurant, High Hesket

The Astra pictured in the days when lorries still thundered up and down the A6 and hundreds of lorry drivers dropped into the transport cafe for a meal and a chat. The cafe was open 24 hours a day and was very popular.

Just after the Second World War Mr and Mrs Fred Counsell along with their partner Mr W J Slater of Carnforth decided to start a small transport cafe on the A6, and it was small. It was little more than a converted chicken house, but the business that they used to cram into it was amazing. In the end it had to be taken down before it fell down.

The first day's takings were 18s 6d (92p) from two lorries and that included the cigarettes the men bought as well. However their hard work soon began to pay off, the cafe became a popular stopping off place and more and more lorries were seen to pull into the large car park.

The transport cafe continued like this for five or six years, and then the restaurant was extended into an old deep litter hen house, which was situated about 70 feet from the cafe. Food was prepared in the kitchen and wheeled over to this new restaurant. In 1963 the 'hen house' restaurant was removed leaving the original cafe and a new extension was built on.

Builder Mr Jack Brunt, of Todhills, won a battle against the severe winter of 1963 with bricks and mortar when he built the Astra Cafe. 'We had to fight the hard frosts all the way,' he said, 'It was a really tough job getting the Astra ready for the summer season, but we did it.'

Mr Fred Counsell had the original idea of using a pre-cast concrete shell. Carlisle architect Mr A F Sewell was called in and soon plans were under way to put the transport cafe on the map. Mr Brunt managed to build the new extension without interfering with the day to day running of the Astra.

The sprung maple dance floor, gleaming stainless steel kitchen and pastel tinted ladies room were all installed by Mr Brunt and his team. Pearsons of Annetwell Street were responsible for the lighting and Boyds of Grape Lane carried out the painting and decorating.

Mr Counsell was extremely proud of the bar, for it conjured up memories of the old Astra. It had the original top from the old serving counter given an up to date look with natural wood. The new restaurant had apex windows, concealed lighting, wall paper from Germany and Scandinavian looking rafters.

The Astra reopened in July 1964 in time for the summer season. In the autumn it rang out with gaiety and music for the Counsells provided an exciting 'Come dance and dine with me' programme. The Astra now boasted a transport cafe, a cafeteria and a restaurant and was run like this until the M6 opened four miles away, when the transport side of the business was closed to make way for coach parties and private motorists.

The silence must have seemed deafening for the first few days after the M6 opened. Distressing as the sudden lack of trade was to Mr Counsell, he had long since forecast the disaster and realised that it was time again to give the Astra a new slant and to cater for the many travellers who he knew would continue to travel on the old road, once the novelty of the motorway had worn off - the coach parties, the tourists, the businessmen and of course the local people out for a meal or an evening's entertainment.

The Astra was closed for a time in 1968 whilst this redecoration was carried out and was reopened on 5 December in time to catch the Christmas trade. With its regular live entertainment the Astra now became one of the largest local roadhouses through the next two decades until it suffered damage from some unfortunate fires. The site is now occupied by a furniture warehouse and salesroom.

Mr Fred Counsell

The 24 hour transport cafe, photographs courtesy of the Cumberland News.

Below the 1968 refurbishment and above an advert to encourage new trade.

The Cameo/the 101 Club and the Talk of the Border, Botchergate

When Mr Dalton's city auction hall, Castle Street came under a compulsory purchase order he moved his business to Botchergate, taking the name City Auction Hall with him.

1940 saw alterations to the venue which had been ran as the City Dance Hall, Botchergate, with the confectioner's shop premises, number 79, being made into an entrance for the dance hall. This venue became known as the Cameo. Through the 1940s Tom Hodgson ran dances there to cater for the troops stationed in the Carlisle area. Music was provided by the Cliff Eland Band with Bobby Laing as resident singer and Rodney Warr as compere.

In the 1960s many alterations were made to the Cameo when it was then converted into the 101 club by Tom with his brother-in-law, Les Leighton as manager. Before going into the ballroom and gaming rooms one passed through a large restaurant, the 101 Steak House, with food provided by the Pioneer Catering Service.

In March 1965 the 101, was advertised as being Carlisle's first night club. Mr H Stewart applied for permission to serve drinks and meals until 1am, saying, 'All other major cities have night clubs. Carlisle

is lagging behind.' A licence was granted for three nights a week - Tuesday, Friday and Saturday, with the option to re-apply for a further extension when the club got on its feet. By November 1965 the 101 nightclub's popularity had risen to such an extent it was now allowed to open six nights a week until 2am. In October 1967 the 101 Club started opening during the day as well as at night serving meals from 5s (25p).

The club was bought by Michael Ewbank, a farmer and butcher from Appleby, in April 1969 and was run under the new name the Talk of the Border with Bunny Girls and gambling providing added attractions.

Both the old 101 Club and the new Talk of the Border were popular venues for local acts as well as famous stars of the era such as Frankie Vaughan, Dickie Valentine, Donald Peers, P J Proby, Lita Rosa and, in the 1970s, a young Freddie Starr, Mud, the Fantastics and Black Lace appeared.

By the late 1970s the club was known as Tiffanys and in 1985 it was given another facelift and a new name, Cheers, later to be followed by Cats Whiskers at which time it was then owned by Almondale (Cumbria) Ltd. The club was destroyed by fire in the late 1990s later being demolished along with other buildings on Botchergate to make way for a new development which took place in 2002/3.

Clockwise from top:

The Butlins 1948 New Year Dance which was held at the Cameo, Botchergate. Charles Amer and his 17 piece dance band provided music for dancing at many Butlins Holiday camps.

Bobby Laing, resident singer for several years at the Cameo Ballroom.

The Cameo band, from left, Ronnie Archibald, John Corson, David Gibson, John Hogarth, Cliff Eland, Ralph Pennington and Eric Duffel.

Clockwise from top:

The 'Find the Singer' contest held at the Cameo in 1962. Pictured, from left, organiser Les Leighton, judges Lyndis Chesney, Michael Cooper and Rodney Warr with centre, the winner, Brian Davis.

Princess Badia, a belly dancer who appeared at the 101 Club in November 1965.

Baked potatoes with your drinks, November 1963, at the Cameo. From left, Heather McKiterick, Linda Walters and Christine Firth

Various adverts for the 101 Club and the Talk of the Border Club from 1the late 1960s including one, centre, following the Club's loss of licence.

Above the 101 Club, 1968, with manager Les Leighton on the left and five members of the VIPs band. Below new owner of the club, Mr Michael Ewbank with manager Rodney Warr.

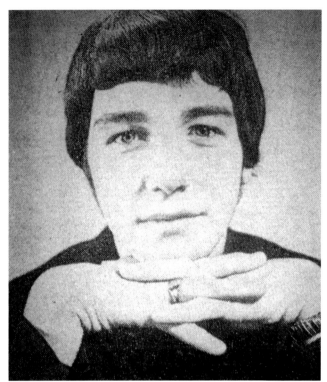

Phil Dee who ran a regular record show at the Talk of the Border Club in 1969.

A group of finalists who took part in the 'Miss Talk of the Border' contest at the club in May 1969.

Long John Baldry who appeared at the Talk of the Border Club in December 1969 and right, Raving Rupert, the UK's answer to Elvis, appearing at the Talk of the Border Club in August 1971.

The Batchelors appearing at the Talk of the Border, December 1969.

Talk of the Border manager Alan Davis, centre, with singer David Whitfield, left, and club director Rodney Warr.

Rodney Warr and Michael Ewbank on their way to see the Royal Command Performance at the Palladium, London, to book acts for a charity function in Carlisle, 1970.

THE PICTURE HOUSES

In the 1950s Carlisle had eight cinemas: the City Pictures House, English Street; the Stanley Hall, the Palace and the Botchergate Picture House, Botchergate; the Public Hall, Chapel Street; the Regal Cinema, Church Street, Caldewgate; the Rex Cinema, Denton Street; the Lonsdale, Warwick Road and the Argyll, Central Avenue, Harraby.

At this time the cinemas would fill early on Thursday and Friday evenings whilst on Saturday nights, with the influx of country people to the town large queues were usually forming by 6pm. However due to the competition and the growth in the popularity of television, there were only three cinemas remaining by the late 1960s and of those only the Lonsdale remains open today.

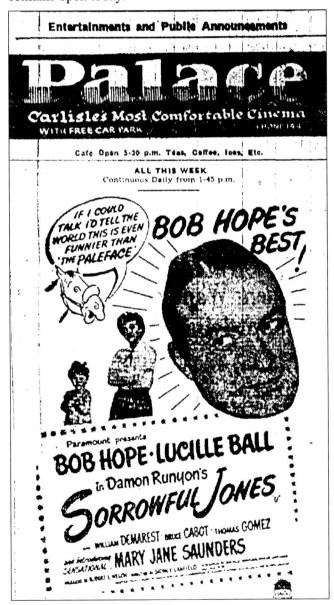

Adverts, above, for films showing at Carlisle cinemas in January 1950.

Just before the First World War a series of cartoons appeared in the *Cumberland News* of men who were prominent in public life in Carlisle at the time. One of these was of Mr Sidney Bacon, the most prominent man in the entertainment business in Carlisle in the early 1900s, who first brought cinema to the city.

Sidney Bacon was from Bishop Auckland,and started his working life helping his father, a photographer, with businesses in Newcastle, Leeds and Liverpool. In his work he met many theatrical people and decided to make the theatre his career. He went into management and had interests in travelling theatrical companies and controlled theatres in Stockton-on-Tees, Newcastle, Gateshead, West Hartlepool and Birmingham before going to London in 1908 to open cinemas.

Realising that moving pictures were the up and coming thing, during the next few years he opened picture houses in Carlisle, Newcastle, York and London. His aim was to provide wholesome programmes of entertainment in comfortable, attractive surrounds and he boasted that there was no programme shown in his picture houses which had not first been viewed and approved by either himself or his manager.

As you will see the background to Zeldir's cartoon shows Her Majesty's Theatre in Lowther street.

Sidney Bacon was there for three years prior to 1915, as the lessee of the theatre. He provided a very good level of entertainment there, but it was at the Public Hall in nearby Chapel Street that his first cinema enterprise in Carlisle began. This was Carlisle's first cinema for the regular showing of moving pictures.

At the Public Hall a children's matinee was held every Saturday, admission being one penny. The films shown were usually cowboys and Indians or stories of the American Civil War with incidental music on the piano when it could be heard above the children's excited shouts.

The Public Hall, Chapel Street. was formerly a chapel or schoolroom built in the 1820s. It was converted into a Public Hall around 1900 and opened as a cinema in 1906. It was closed in 1956 and the hall then passed to retail use. Photograph courtesy of Carlisle Library.

The City Picture House, English Street

Sidney Bacon did not build the cinema in English Street which stood on the site of the present Marks and Spencer's store (formerly Littlewoods) but about a year after it was built he bought it and changed its name to the City Picture Houe. Carlisle's first purpose built cinema, modest in size and fittings, compared with many later giants, was considered the last word in luxury when it opened in 1915.

A brochure prepared for the opening ceremony performed by Alderman Walter P Gibbings on 4 November 1915, describes the building and its furnishings in glowing terms.

The City Picture House, English Street, photograph courtesy of the Carlisle Journal.

The Cinema on English Street was built by the local firm of J and R Bell to the design of London architects. A feature of the cream coloured facade was the open balcony on the first floor. Inside the emphasis was on oak in the foyer and tea room above, while the main hall was in the style of Louis XVI with an enriched ceiling and cornice supported by pillars and the walls in dark wood with tapestry panels.

The oak room cafe at the City Picture House was a very popular meeting place in the 20s and 30s, under the management of the late Bertha Shaw. The tables on the balcony gave a wonderful view of all that was going on in the centre of the town and this attempt at outdoor eating in the continental style was very popular in the summer time.

Not long after its opening it was bought by Mr Sidney Bacon, who boasted, 'Here you will find comedies containing much wholesome mirth, but no vulgarity, dramas minus the objectionable features too often allied with photo plays, but plus a powerful and well sustained interest, pictures from which you will learn much that is going on in the world of science, art, commerce, topical pictures both local and general. You will get entertainment and amusement plus information, education and breadth of outlook that will inspire you and give you topics of conversation, things to think or to talk about.'

Of course there was also music which was provided by an orchestra of first class musicians playing music chosen to suit the pictures being shown. The cheapest seats at this time were 4d (2p).

The City Picture House came under the control of ABC in 1937 and ran under them as a subsidiary to the newer Lonsdale. It was closed on the 18 June 1960.

The annual Christmas party for the City Picture House held at the Top Hat cafe.

The Palace Cinema, Botchergate

When it was opened in 1906 it was known as the Palace Theatre. In 1909 it was leased to Frank MacNaughton and became known as the New Palace Theatre and ran Cine-Variety from that date. The cinematograph license lapsed around the war years of 1914-1918 at which time it returned to live theatre. By 1933 Carlisle could no longer support two theatres so it was fitted with talking picture equipment and became a full time cinema. By 1950 a cafe was being advertised at the cinema and prices for the pictures at this time were 9d and 2/3d.

A presentation at the City Picture House in February 1950 to Mr E J Harrington, assistant manager who had been appointed to a similar post at the Lonsdale Cinema. Photograph courtesy of Carlisle Journal.

The Palace Cinema, photograph courtesy of the Cumberland News, 1958.

The Palace Cinema foyer, picture courtesy of Tullie House.

In September 1950 Mr George Fishwick, manager of the Palace Cinema left to take up a new position in London. He was replaced by Mr A V Spathaky.

In August 1970 the Palace Cinema became Studios 1 and 2 under the management of Mr Jack Morris (left). Photograph courtesy of the Carlisle Journal.
Mr Bill Carruthers, manager of Studios 1, 2, 3 & 4 (right)

In 1972 in what was hailed as one of the most ambitious and advanced projects of its kind, Carlisle became the first city in the North of England to have a four Cinema Centre with the opening of the luxurious studios 1,2,3 & 4, complex. The cinema finally closed on 1 March 1987 and was later converted into the United Services Club (formerly of Cecil St.). The building is now empty.

Above Mr George Fisher and Mr A V Spathaky. and below the queue at the Palace Cinema to see 'South Pacific' in August 1960.

The Botchergate Picture House

It must have been quite a race in 1915, as to which of the two new cinemas, the City Picture House or the Botchergate Picture House, would open first. The Botchergate Picture House was first used as a Wesleyan Chapel annex on Sundays. By 1922 it was being advertised as the Picture House, Cinema & Cafe. It acquired equipment for 'Talkies' in 1929. By 1956 it had been renamed the Gaumont and later became the Odeon.

Geoff Dickens recalls that the lads would arrange to meet their girlfriends outside the cinema and, as it was opposite the Cumberland Pub, the lads would sit upstairs and keep watch out of the window for the girls who were waiting in the queue. When they were nearly at the front the lads would down their drinks and join them.

The cinema was closed by its new owners Rank in 1969 due to competition. The site is at present being developed into new entertainment venues.

Pictured below the Botchergate Picture House, photograph courtesy of Carlisle Library.

Above an advert for the Gaumont's programme from the Carlisle Journal, August 1956 and below Carlisle's Mayor joins the children of the Gaumont Boys and Girls Club. Photograph courtesy of the Cumberland News.

The sweet counter at the Gaumont in June 1962. Photograph courtesy of Carlisle Library.

The Rex Cinema, Denton Street

The Rex Cinema was formerly the Star Hall with a billiard hall attached. Sound equipment was fitted in 1930 and around 1938 the cinema was re-named the Rex. By the 1960s bingo was becoming popular and the building was mainly used as a bingo and social club although it was still showing some films. The cinema side finally ended in 1970 when it was given over entirely to bingo, for which it is still popular today.

The Rex Cinema, photograph courtesy of Carlisle Library.

The Stanley Hall, Botchergate

This was built in 1906 as part of a complex of auction marts for John Harrison, with a hall above. It was first used as a skating rink and dance hall, but began showing films around 1910. The cinema was closed on 3 January 1959. After a time as a dance hall it was then converted into the Stanley Hall flats.

The Regal Cinema, Caldewgate

This was originally a chapel building, which opened as a cinema in 1930. It closed in the mid 1960s and was converted into a bingo hall.

The Regal Cinema, Caldewgate, in 1974. Photograph courtesy of Carlisle Library.

The Lonsdale, Warwick Road

The Lonsdale was built on the site of a property which had been destroyed in a large fire, giving the owners a perfect chance to have a cinema in the centre of the city. Built for Sidney Bacon's Pictures Ltd. the Lonsdale was certainly an eye opener for the city audiences of the day.

The cinema opened on 21 September 1931 for pictures and variety shows. The Lonsdale was the largest of Carlisle's cinemas, having a seating capacity of 2000. In those days the music of the mighty Christie organ played by Harold Meredith filled the place.

The Lonsdale has changed hands several times. It was taken over from its original owners Sidney Bacon Pictures Ltd in about 1940 by Union Cinemas. In 1962 it was then bought from them by the ABC group who became part of the EMI organisation. The Lonsdale was managed by Mr Norman Scott Buccleugh from 1955 to 1972.

During the post war boom the Lonsdale had a weekly turnover of 30,000 people but by 1970 they were lucky to get 5000 through the doors each week. In

An artist's impression of the Lonsdale Cinema, opened in 1931. Drawing courtesy of the Cumberland News.

was by now also showing several film premieres.

The cinema closed in 1972 and was reopened with part of the building for bingo. In 1978 the cinema was twinned, a third screen being added in October 1987. In 1993 a new cinema was opened and was ran in conjunction with the Lonsdale Cinema. This is still a cinema and bingo hall .

An advert for the opening of the Lonsdale Cinema.

these post war years through to 1969 the Lonsdale saw many famous names on stage with some, like Cliff Richard appearing on more than one occasion.

In one 1963 show the bill featured the Beatles who were well down the bill and not to prove so popular, along with Helen Shapiro and Danny Williams, of *Moon River* fame and Kenny Lynch, with Des O'Conner as the compare. It was a different matter the next time the Beatles appeared at the Lonsdale, for by then they had taken the pop world by storm. The box office opened on a Saturday morning for the advance sale of tickets and a queue began to form as early as the previous Wednesday evening. By Friday it stretched way down to Tait Street. Beatle Mania had hit Carlisle.

The Rolling Stones appeared on 17 September 1964 and again in October 1965, when they kept an eager audience waiting for ten minutes, due to their vehicle breaking down. In 1967 guitar legend Jimi Hendrix appeared, sharing the stage with the Walker Brothers, Cat Stephens and Englebert Humperdinck. The latter being the last big star to grace the stage in 1969, alongside Mary Hopkin, who was making her first personal appearance, after her hit *Those were the Days* had been at number one in the charts.

On the film side of the Lonsdale, January 1954 saw the beginning of the three stages of 'operation entertainment' with the introduction of 3-D to Carlisle for the first time in December 1954. The second stage was the introduction of the panoramic views of Cinema Scope and the third stage took place in January 1955 when the Lonsdale became the only cinema in the county to have stereophonic sound. It was also the first to start a children's Saturday morning shows and

The interior of the Lonsdale, photograph courtesy of Carlisle Library.

Two adverts from autumn 1954 for films at the Lonsdale.

Some of the stars who appeared at the ABC Lonsdale in the 1950s, including the Beverley Sisters, Dicky Valentine, Frankie Vaughan and Max Bygraves.

The Lonsdale in the 1940s when it was run by Union Cinemas. Photograph courtesy of Carlisle Library.

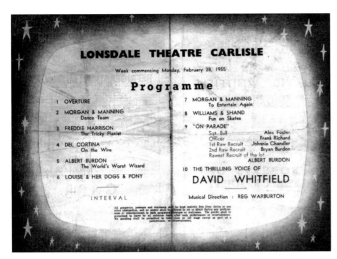

A programme of events for the Lonsdale Theatre from February 1955, courtesy of Tommy Giacopazzi.

Celebrating its 25th anniversary in September 1956 the cake's maker Mr J McGillivray-Smith (right) meets the ABC Cinema's manager, Mr. Scott Buccleugh.

Above Jean Nichol and Carol Talmage meet Cliff Richard, October 1959.
Below August 1957 and queues of Tommy Steele fans wait outside the Lonsdale Cinema for the film of his life story.

Marty Wilde top of the bill at the Lonsdale, meets Norma Johnstone, Joyce Parkinson and Dorothy Blanchard in February 1960.

Carlisle Grammar School boys, Leon Pollock, Stephen Beattie and Michael Hollingsworth meet Cliff Richard at the Lonsdale in May 1960.

Cliff Richard with Lonsdale ABC manager Norman Scott-Buccleugh (third left) and other artistes at the performance in 1960.

Billy Fury who played at the Lonsdale in November 1961.

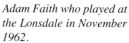
Adam Faith who played at the Lonsdale in November 1962.

Above Lorraine Jaynes meets her favourite star Helen Shapiro at the Lonsdale in February 1963.

Beatle mania came to Carlisle in October 1963 when youngsters queued for 36 hours before tickets went on sale for the November concert. Alan Gordon and David Little are pictured below waiting for the ticket office to open.

Police struggle to control the stampede when the ticket office finally opens. The police chain was broken and in the rush to get to the ticket office some people were injured.

The lights go down, the curtains go up and yes, it's the Beatles.

St John's Ambulance Brigade members treat one of the casualties.

Above Gerry and the Pacemakers at the ABC.

Right January 1965, Chuck Berry played at the ABC Cinema along with the Moody Blues.

The Beatles, November 1963 at the Lonsdale.

The Rolling Stones came to Carlisle on 17 September 1964 and fans mobbed them when they arrived at the ABC Lonsdale. One of the group had a handful of hair pulled from his head by a girl.

Ambulances were called several times as fans fainted during performances. One girl was taken to hospital twice - once before her heroes had even arrived.

The screams of the fans echoed through Carlisle as girls drifted away, singing snatches of pop tunes and occasionally giving isolated high pitched squeals of delight.

Before the group arrived the crowds were described as, 'Quite small and orderly', but between the shows they swelled as queues formed for the second performance and passers by stopped to stare.

The band were ten minutes late as their car had broken down on the M6. Mick Jagger said, 'I think the fan belt broke and cut through something.' Keith Richards added, 'When the AA man arrived, he told us he hadn't the spare parts, so he told the police and they arranged a hire car.'

Two police dogs were on patrol outside and inside the Lonsdale a security guard had to stop fans from climbing onto the stage.

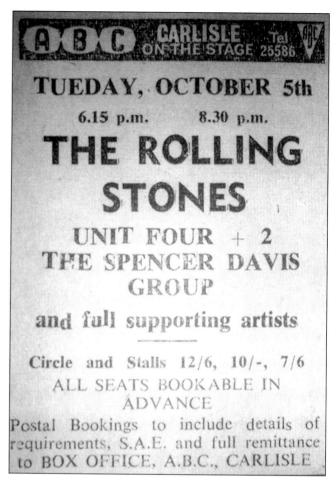

Christine Blythe and Dorothy Lamb of Carlisle meet their pop hero, Mick Jagger.

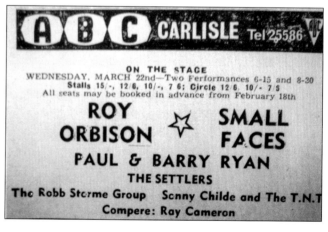

The Stones in Carlisle, after their breakdown on the M6.

Roy Orbison

Jimi Hendrix, Cat Stephens, Engelbert Humperdinck and the Walker Brothers appeared at the ABC in April 1967.

April 1971 and manager of the ABC Cinema Norman Scott Buccleugh is pictured outside the cinema which was soon after divided to provide space for bingo.

Engelbert Humperdinck and Mary Hopkins who appeared at the ABC in March 1969.

May Nixon (centre) with Fiona Docherty and Liz Stephenson. May retired in June 2003, aged 84. She had worked in cinemas all her life, starting at the City Picture House, English Street, then the Palace, Botchergate and finally moving to the Lonsdale after the Palace closed.

The Argyll Cinema and the Cosmo, Central Avenue, Harraby

Mr A C Roy, architect (centre), Mr R Bell and Mr W Bell (managing director) discuss the plans for the Argyll Cinema.

The Argyll.

Below youngsters outside the newly-opened Argyll Cinema at Harraby, in 1956.

ARGYLL CINEMA
HARRABY. PHONE 21492
Carlisle's Most Modern Cinema.   Free Car Park—250 Cars.

GRAND GALA OPENING
MONDAY, 23rd JULY, 6.30 p.m.
BY THE WORSHIPFUL THE MAYOR
COUNCILLOR RITSON GRAHAM, J.P.

20th
Century-Fox presents
RODGERS & HAMMERSTEIN'S
CAROUSEL
EASTMAN COLOUR
THE FIRST
CINEMASCOPE 55
PICTURE

Starring GORDON MacRAE · SHIRLEY JONES
with CAMERON MITCHELL

THE OPENING FILM WILL RUN SIX DAYS, THEREAFTER THE PROGRAMMES WILL CHANGE TWICE WEEKLY
Normal Daily Opening Times—Cont. from approx. 1.30 p.m.
Sunday, Continuous from 5 p.m.   Doors Open 4.30 p.m.
Special Children's Matinee Every Saturday morning, at 10 a.m. Doors open 9.30
CINEMA PRICES (inc. Tax)
Rear Stalls, 2/9; Centre Stalls, 2/2; Front Stalls, 1/6.
Old Age Pensioners, 7d.
SPECIAL SATURDAY MORNING CHILDREN'S MATINEE 6d

The Argyll was the first cinema to open in Carlisle since 1931. It was built for the people of Carlisle's new satellite city of Harraby, which was being built at the time, bringing motion pictures to the door steps of the suburb's residents thus cutting out their long journey into the town centre and also alleviating the problems of the build up of queues in the town, particularly on weekends.

The Argyll Cinema was opened on Monday 23 July 1956 with a seating capacity for around 1000. It was run by Rural Cinema and Entertainments Ltd. and the

Managing director was Mr William Bell, of Scotby Road. Ticket prices were from 1s 6d to 2s 9d.

Due to falling audiences it closed its doors only three years later in October 1959. After extensive refurbishment including a new floor being laid, well above the level of the old cinema floor the building reopened in October 1960, as the Cosmo Rollarena, a combined dance venue and roller skating rink. Another two years later and the building became a victim of the bingo craze.

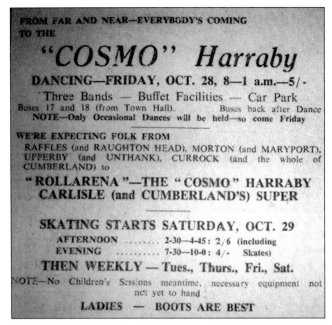

The Argyll Cinema converted into a roller skating and dance floor.

The Cosmo as a bingo hall.

Members of the staff of Border Enterprises at their annual party in the Cosmo.

After the bingo craze dwindled slightly the ballroom and club came into existence. Previously the management held popular dances in the Crown and Mitre Ballroom but when Trust House took over the hotel dances were transferred to the Cosmo, with the enticement of free buses and a free meal. The Cosmo was initially run by the Hodgson family, with Sandra Hodgson becoming the wife of Les Leighton who became the manager of the club. There was certainly a lot of work to be done and patrons who had seen the club and ballroom when it first opened in 1960 noticed a big difference by January 1966, after extensive alterations had been made.

The floor level of the old cinema made it possible to include many unique features in the building. At one end there was a basement bar, with the stage situated about three quarters of the way up the hall, then at the other end of the dance floor there was a staircase to the 'Sky Top' bar, where the first pop group appeared. A genuine maple floor was fitted at a cost of around £3000. There was no room left inside the building, so further extensions had to be added.

Learning a roller skate 'snake' dance.

Kitchens were added so the club could develop its catering facilities, taking 75 private bookings in that first year. There was also the Pennine Bar with many alcoves, where romance would take place.

The Cosmo became not only the local pop Mecca, but probably the social hub of Carlisle during the 1960s and 70s with hordes of clubbers coming from all over Cumbria for a night out. The club hosted not only local bands mentioned in this book, but also those who would go on to become some of the biggest names in pop and rock.

There were six bars, with 29 bar staff, and 11 glass collectors, doing nothing but collecting glasses all night. In its heyday it had around 19,000 members and you couldn't get in unless you had your membership card. Many people remember it well as the place they met their future spouses. Les Leighton sold the club in 1974 and moved to Spain, but its legend has refused to die.

Director Les Leighton and his wife, Sandra, who was also well known as an artist and painted groups such as the Moody Blues.

Bottom of page Gerry and the Pacemakers when they appeared at the Cosmo.

Sitting out between dances to 'The Sessionaires' at the Cosmo in October 1963, are from left, Maureen Leach, Lucy Young, Valerie Wilson and Wendy Armstrong.

WHERE DO YOU FIND CUMBERLAND'S FINEST BALLROOM?

MAPLE FLOOR · SPECIAL LIGHTING EFFECTS
BANQUETS · BUFFETS · SNACKS
SIX BEAUTIFULLY APPOINTED BARS
FREE CAR PARK (250 CARS) ADJOINING
NEW WELL APPOINTED LADIES' POWDER ROOMS

IN FACT EVERYTHING THAT AN ORGANISATION REQUIRES FOR A DANCE, DINNER, CONCERT, MEETING, WEDDING, TRADE SHOW, etc.

Above Georgie Fame and the Blue Flames at the Cosmo.

THIS SUNDAY

GEORGIE FAME
and the
BLUE FLAMES

PLUS
Scotland's
Fabulous
SABRES

8-0 to 11-30—
10/-

AT THE COSMO THIS SUNDAY

The Cosmo hosted Liverpool group Lee Castle and the Barons.

Right, Deep Purple who played at the Cosmo in the 1960s.

61

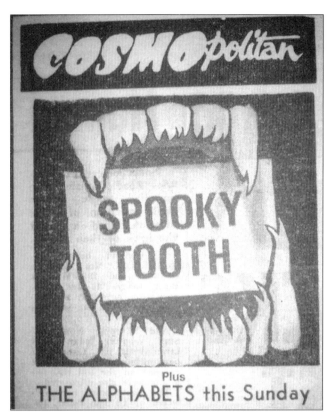

Some of the members and friends of the Carlisle and Border RSCDS enjoying themselves at their annual ball at the Cosmo.

The Cosmo in 1970

EARLY 60S ENTERTAINMENT

Carlisle's first Chinese restaurant opened in March 1960. It is now the Shaha Indian restaurant.

The King's Hall was refurbished and opened as a youth centre in September 1961 and adverts for a 'night on the town' from 1964.

The Central Hotel, Victoria Viaduct, cashed in on the success of the Cavern and started its own cellar bar with music in January 1965. Photograph courtesy of the Carlisle Journal.

The Langley Hall Hotel, Corby Hill, became a popular place to eat when it opened in December 1965. The hostess was Mrs Carole Tranter, pictured right.

THE BATS

The Border Artistes Theatrical Society was formed in 1967 at a meeting in the Red Lion Hotel, called by Rodney Warr and Richie Jefferson. It was proposed that a society be formed for charitable purposes with local artistes invited to join and give their services for fund raising concerts.

Rob Tower was elected president. The Towers family had cinemas in Gretna, Eastriggs, Annan, Lockerbie and took over the Lonsdale when ABC pulled out. Rodney Warr was elected 'King Bat' in 168-9 and in subsequent years the honour went to Frank Logan, Tommy Kennedy, Dai Watkins, Jerry Johnstone, Dennis Mitchell and Ritchie Jefferson. Mr Jefferson, as treasurer, had the title of 'vampire bat'.

The original members of the Border Artistes Theatrical Society, founded in 1967, pictured below. Back from left, Richard Jefferson, Tom Lomas and Rodney Warr. Centre, Jean Johnstone, Reuben Slater, Tommy Kennedy, Charlie Blake and Bobby Laing. Front, Jimmy and Brian Slater and Arthur Belcher, who with Reuben Slater, were Rue and the Rockets.
The BATS held a gala concert at HM Theatre in December 1968. Pictured from left are Rodney Warr, Rue Slater and Bill Gore, pictured above right

Lady members were called 'Queen bats'. Peter Hoban was the 'King Bat' in the organisation's final year. to good causes including buying a caravan for needy families to have holidays at Silloth. They also bought a music system for the Kinmount Pensioners Centre in memory of Bobby Laing and they paid for the training of a guide dog for the blind.

The BATS variety concerts were hit by the rise in pop music and the final event took place at the Coach House, Heads Nook, in September 1982.

Tommy Kennedy.

Members of the BATS at a rehearsal for their charity show in October 1969, from left, Larry Vickers, Jean Johnston, Rodney Warr, Dae Watkins, Herbert Vickers and Frank Logan with Tom Kennedy in front.

Billy Gore, December 1968

The BATS in 1971, standing from left, Howard Midgely, Frank Logan, Gerry Johnstone, Dai Watkins (King Bat), Dennis Mitchell, Richard Jefferson (Vampire Bat), Tommy Kennedy. Front, Laura Metcalfe, Rob Towers (president), Rodney Warr, Jean Johnstone (Queen Bat).

The BATS going off on their annual summer trip but they decide to pull the bus!

Members of the BATS toasting retiring Bat King and Queen Rodney Warr and Jean Johnston at the first annual dinner and dance of the BATS in the Crown & Mitre Hotel, April 1969.

Tommy Kennedy and Stan McManus, who both served as King Bat, seen here at the Lido, Silloth in the 1970s.

Former Queen Bat, Jean Johnston and Ethel Galloway, whose husband took his turn as King Bat, either side of Pete Hoban, King Bat in 1981/2. The King Bat wore a special sash with a bat logo made from brass plate re-claimed from HMS Ark Royal when she was brought in to be scrapped.

THE COUNTRY PUBS

The Helk Moon, Barclose, Scaleby in 1962. The building has since been demolished to make way for a housing estate. Photograph courtesy of Cumbria Heritage.

During the 1960s the country pub scene was vibrant with each venue having its own resident musicians, some with single acts and the larger venues with duos or trios.

The evening's entertainment would begin with the resident musicians and then the 'sing-a-long' would get under way. There was never a shortage of singers or comedians to join because professionals, semi-professionals and amateurs alike would frequent these venues. These were the equivalent of the modern day Karaoke evenings.

The Golden Fleece, Ruleholme used to host Molly Douglas, who was one of the earliest musicians at Ruleholme and the Maurice Petry Trio.

The Royal Oak, Sebergham had entertainment from Geoff Dickens and Gordon Atkinson as compere and Tommy Baxter on the organ.

The Red Lion, Cumwitton hosted Ronnie Atkinson on accordion and also Dennis Westmorland who in 1973 started the Country Rovers and became well known at Hunt balls, Young Farmers' dances and village hall functions. He is still playing today.

At Dalston Hall you could hear the Tommy Giacopazzi Trio and Tommy Kennedy as compere and at the Helk Moon, Bar Close, Scaleby, David Clapperton and later Gil Johnston, who in the 1980s led the Gillbilliess.

The singers, often had favourite songs, for instance, Shirley Slee - *Stand by Your Man*; Keith Patterson - *Avanagaila*; Ronnie Irving - *She wears Red Feathers*; Bobby Jackson - *Spinning Wheel*; Ian Hunter - *Distant Drums*; Billy Hunter - *Scottish Soldier*; Ronnie Lowther - *Puppet on a String* and Ronnie Shaw - *Little Arrows*.

Also further venues ensured that there was work for

all concerned at Scotby, Sour Nook, Calthwaite, Low Row, Moota, Gilcrux and many more.

The breathalyser was taken more seriously than the 3d per go reaction meters, which were seen to be nothing more than a gimmick when State Management installed them in the pubs in 1960.

In May 1962 an advert appeared in the *Carlisle Journal* to encourage drinkers to visit pubs in the country such as the Crown Hotel and the Hare and Hounds, Wigton; the Golden Fleece, Ruleholme; the White Hart Hotel, Brampton; the New Inn, Milton; the Greenhead Hotel, Gilsland; Haywain Inn, Little Corby; String of Horses, Faugh; Hare and Hounds, Talkin; Weary Sportsman, Castle Carrock; Blue Bell Inn, Newbiggin; Cross Keys, High Hesket; Travellers Rest, Cowrigg and the Royal Oak, Sour Nook.

A customer in the Caledonian State Inn, Botchergate, tries the new reaction meter.

The Golden Fleece, Ruleholme

The Golden Fleece, Ruleholme, near Brampton, was one of the largest roadhouses in the county and was closely associated with the Maurice Petry Trio. In 1968 the large music room at the Golden Fleece had to be closed due to a fall in trade because of the effect of the breathalyser law. However at this time the new management, Gerry and Sheila Thompson offered the use of this room to any artiste or band wanting to rehearse.

The Golden Fleece staff and friends, including the Maurice Petry Trio.

The Maurice Petry Trio, from left, Tom Lomas, Richard 'Ritchie' Jefferson and Maurice Petry, pictured in the 1960s at the Golden Fleece.

Pictured at the Golden Fleece, from left, Arthur Belcher and on far right, Pete Batey (bass player with Junkyard Angel) and Maurice Petry.

Maurice Petry and Charlie Blake, the name of the lady in the centre is not known.

Drag artist Terry Durham who appeared at the Golden Fleece.

The photograph below was taken in December 1971 at a gala variety night in aid of the Evening News and Star Christmas Appeal held at the Golden Fleece, Ruleholme. From left, back, John Hetherington, Tom Lomas, David Carrick, trumpet player; Stewart Jesset, bass player with Gentlemen of Jazz; Pete Watson, bass with Johnnie Duncan and the Bluegrass Boys; Kenny Fitzpatrick, tenor. Front, unknown, Maurice Petry, Mrs Norma Baxter and Paul Baxter.

Molly Douglas, aged 65, who played the organ at the Golden Fleece, pictured here with John Hope (guitar) and Eric Wood (drums).

in Aid of "EVENING NEWS and STAR"
CHRISTMAS APPEAL FOR OLD FOLK

GRAND
VARIETY CONCERT
(Produced by RODNEY WARR)
At the GOLDEN FLEECE, RULEHOLME
WEDNESDAY, 29th NOVEMBER, at 8 p.m.
Admission 3/-
(Tickets, strictly limited, at Golden Fleece and
"Cumberland News" Office)
Great Variety Bill, Topped by —
RODNEY WARR with RUE and THE ROCKETS
Giving Services Free in Aid of Pensioners' Fund

Comedian Charlie Blake who appeared at the Golden Fleece.

Entertainers at the Golden Fleece, Bobby Laing, Tommy Kennedy and Jean Johnston.

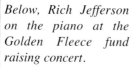

Left, Rodney Warr who did his 'Frankie Vaughan' act at the Golden Fleece.

Below, Rich Jefferson on the piano at the Golden Fleece fund raising concert.

In February 1969 the Golden Fleece was presented with the Evening News & Star's shield for licensed premises who raised most money for charity. Singer Anne Shelton, pictured here with Rodney Warr, presented the shield.

Singing star Anne Shelton sang at the Golden Fleece before presenting the winning shield to Will and Norma Baxter, with Lynn Elliott, assistant editor of the Evening News & Star on the left.

The Border Terrier, Morton

Giving a helping hand at the new Border Terrier pub, are Pam Crellin and Elaine Wallace.

Pulling the first pint at the Border Terrier.

The Carlisle and District State Management Scheme's answer to the breathalyser was the Border Terrier, Morton. The pub, built at a cost of around £50,000 was opened on Wednesday 16 August 1967 when a top home office official pressed the button for the first pint to be pulled.

The Terrier embraced all the qualities of a roadhouse, for in the 150-seater lounge bar the State laid on an £1100 electric organ, a ballroom floor, stage and piped music to add to the normal drinking amenities.

The manager, Mr Harry Crellin believed that when the more stringent laws concerning drinking and driving came into effect, customers would be reluctant to drive to the country pubs. 'This is where the Border Terrier will score' he said, 'we are on a bus route, and taxi fares are quite cheap from the centre of the city. An excellent evening's entertainment will be handy for anyone in the city.'

With the opening of the Terrier a new scene unfolded. The large concert room was regularly packed to the door with 400 or 500 people. After talking to the locals we discovered that it wasn't just the flash surroundings they came to see. It was the entertainment provided by the electric organ and the local artistes, like Maurice Petry, Brian Davis and compere/singer, Jim 'Jazzer' Boyle. This venue was soon known as one of the best in the area with most of the 1960s entertainers mentioned in this book performing there at one time or another.

The smoke room bar, decorated in scarlet and black. In direct contrast to Carlisle's old style 'spit and sawdust' bar rooms the public bar at the Border Terrier was modern, light, airy and well furnished. The Evening News & Star said that the pub was 'thronged with customers' when it first opened.

Some of the performers who took part in a concert at the Border Terrier in aid of the Evening News and Star old folks Christmas Appeal Fund in December 1968. The entertainment was provided by the Travellers, Johnny Alone Trio and the Terriers' resident musicians.

Compere/singer Jim 'Jazzer' Boyle, pictured centre, is a well known personality with 40 years' experience in charity functions. Jazzer compered at the Border Terrier in its heyday. Later he worked at the Pirelli Club which was opened in December 1973.

71

COUNTRY MUSIC

Country music is sometimes mistakenly called Country & Western, however the latter is derived from much earlier music from 1930s America and Hollywood singing cowboys such as Roy Rogers. (Bill C Malone's *Country Music USA* covers the history of the past 50 years of Country & Western music for those readers who are avid fans).

The 1950s in Britain saw the rise in popularity of 'skiffle', a sort of do-it-yourself country music played on home made instruments like the washboard and the chest double bass. The king of skiffle was the legendary Lonnie Donegan.

Many artists both local and international had their roots in skiffle before moving into the new sound of Rock 'n Roll. Mick Jagger, as a 15-year-old schoolboy wrote in an essay titled *How to form a Skiffle Group*, 'Before any group is started up there should be someone who can sing really well and a couple of guitarists who can play good strong chords.'

Among the first skiffle groups in Carlisle were the Terry Degnan Skiffle Group, with singer Lindy Rum (today Lindy Waddell of Harraby), who after personnel changes went on to be the Four Dollars and Dave Batey's Zenith Skiffle Group.

King of skiffle, Lonnie Donegan and Norman Scott-Buccleugh at the Lonsdale ABC in 1957.

A professional group of cowboys - the Terry Degnan Skiffle Group.

The Terry Degnan Skiffle Group on stage at Her Majesty's Theatre during a 1950s country show extravaganza.

Although most of the acts were initially influenced by skiffle and country music they moved on to leave the more dedicated to specialise. Country music did not take off in Carlisle at this time but it was very popular in West Cumbria at venues such as the Lofthouse Motel, Bothel with the Lofthouse Cowboys and the Saddlers.

New Season's Attractions at
LOFTHOUSE MOTEL
BOTHEL
ON THE COCKERMOUTH/CARLISLE ROAD
In the Western Room
Sundays
OPEN TALENT COMPETITION
Come along and compete for grand final.
All types of acts welcome.
Heat winners £5.   Grand final winner £25.
First heats: Sunday, November 9th, 1969
Wednesdays
PARTY NIGHT
Dancing to the LOFTHOUSE COWBOYS
Party games, forfeits, party sing along.
Snacks and Dinners served each evening.
Licensed Bars.
Open daily, except Monday, 9 a.m. to 12 midnight.
9 a.m. Morning Coffee (home baked scones & cakes)
12 noon Lunches, choice of menu.
3 p.m. Afternoon Teas and High Teas.
7 p.m. Dinners, choice of menu.
Entertainment in Western Room.
MUSIC and DANCING Every Night Except Monday

Pictured below, the Lofthouse Cowboys - Derek Tolson, Dennis Blamire, Tony Renney and vocalist Chris Graham.

The Saddlers, standing from left, Derek Tolson, Ken Kirby and Tony Renney with Chris Graham and Colin Wright.

In the early 1960s country music began to become more popular in Carlisle with acts such as Mel Adams and Gil Johnston, who in 1980 formed the Gillbillies. There was also Jackie Atkinson, Geoff Dickens, Mike Baxter, Red Skelton, the Drifting Cowboys with Malcolm Mason who went on to form Lemongrass in 1967. Other popular acts were Doreen Duncan, who in 1972 became part of Country Breeze, Dennis Westmorland, and ex-Hotrod's guitarist Phil Bayne who played with Pam Donabie as the Runaways, along with Pete Hoban who joined the band in 1969.

Gil Johnston, country compere and vocalist.

73

Pam Donabie of Gretna and Phil Bayne, Carlisle, who presented a programme of country and western numbers at a concert in Her Majesty's Theatre in 1967.

Three of the 1967 line up of Lemon Grass, from left, Dave Little, ex-VIP Walter Johnstone and Malcolm Mason. Missing from this picture was Mike Wilding. The name came when one of the band bought a tin of talc called 'Lemon Grass'.

The Drifting Cowboys in the mid-1960s, with Dave Scotson on drums, Dave Storey and Malcolm Mason at the Golden Fleece, Ruleholme.

By the late 1960s the popularity of country music had risen to such an extent to warrant a full show. On Saturday 8 May 1968 country and western fans in Cumbria came in for a veritable feast of talent when a complete American show visited Carlisle with an all star cast of top US names in country music.

The Johnny Cash Show visited the ABC Lonsdale theatre for one night only. Of special interest to both fans of country and rock was Carl Perkins, who was the original recorder of Elvis Presley's *Blue Suede Shoes*. Other acts included June Carter who sang with Johnny Cash and recorded many successful numbers with him, the Statler Brothers of *Flowers on the Wall* fame, and the Tennessee Three.

As the popularity of country music grew so did the number of venues offering evenings of country. These included Langley Hall, Lazonby Village Hall, the Astra, the Crown at Low Hesket, Port Carlisle Caravan Park and the Grey Hound Inn at Bothel. In fact most of the country pub venues offered entertainers or sing-a-longs to country music. The early 1970s saw new venues made available to cater for country fans such as the Peacock Room at Newby Grange, opened in 1973.

Country Breeze formed in 1972 comprised of lead vocalist Doreen Duncan, lead guitarist, Alan Sessford, rhythm guitarist, Ian Mitchell and drummer Bob

74

Duncan. The four from Dumfries had all been on the scene during the 1960s doing their own different things. At the time they were described as being Britain's zephyr of country music - a gentle and mild west-wind capable of rising with the occasional gust to whip up the mood of their material.

They were much in demand at leading cabaret clubs in the Borders area of Scotland and the North of England. Occasionally, when bookings permitted, they enjoyed guest appearances in touring shows such as those headed by the Alexander Brothers and Johnny Beattie and the Hillsiders.

The Runaways Country Band in the earlier 1990s. Standing from left, Ken Bowman, Phil Bayne and Bob Hinkley with Ali Bayne, Pam Bayne and Dave Midgely.

In this 1980s line up of Country Breeze, standing are Bob Duncan, and Tony Renney with Ian Duncan, Doreen Duncan and ex-Dolls' Dennis Watt.

The Gillbillies namely Stan MacManus, Dave Midgely, Tommy Giacopazzi, Gill Johnston and Howard Midgely were originally brought together by Gil Johnston as a fun band at the Solway Lido, Silloth. Photograph courtesy of Tommy Giacopazzi.

Jazz

By the mid 1950s jazz was seen to be coming into its own, even becoming respectable. What was once called with a sneer, 'African Jungle Music' was now being recognised as something very different - a modern art form of American origin, which expressed moods and emotions foreign to nearly all other forms of music. Over the early months of 1954 jazz was becoming more popular and was the trend record makers were watching with the greatest interest.

One of Carlisle's popular early 1950s venues for this new sound was the Top Hat Club, Blackfriars Street. Another venue, which became a mecca for Carlisle jazz enthusiasts, was the Garrett Club, which was above the Wonder Milk Bar at number 20 Devonshire Street. Every Tuesday night it was the same, subdued lighting in a room with its walls covered with murals and a group of inspired musicians obscured by the dim Bohemian atmosphere. They were watched by an audience of young people, not Bobby Soxers, Spivs and Teddy Boy s, but ordinary girls and boys who, after a busy day's work would go to relax and socialise. On Sunday nights jazz music was followed by an illustrated lecture on the history of jazz.

According to a jazz club tradition a former occupant of the Garrett had hung himself there at the turn of the century (1900). Once a year they say that the shadow of the noose can be seen swaying on the wall and if you were lucky enough you would see a figure swinging from it.

Jazz at the Garrett Club was founded in the autumn of 1954 and was home to two local bands - Mick Potts with his Gateway Jazz Band and the Arthur Curwen Group.

In a bid to attract youngsters the early 1960s also saw the introduction of a Jazz Club Night into the then failing Her Majesty's Theatre, although this was not as well supported as it might have been.

In January 1963 the licensee of the Kings Head, Mr John Ellerton offered the Carlisle Jazz Club part of his pub for Sunday evening sessions. The old world Kings Head Tavern rocked with rhythm with the opening of the city's new jazz club. Music was by four of Carlisle's top jazz bands - the Arthur Curwen Trio with singers Rhonda and Jackie Atherton, the Black Tulip Orchestra, Trombones Incorporated and the Downbeat 4.

Within six weeks the membership grew to such an extent that the Kings Head grew too small and new premises had to be found. Carlisle and District State Management offered the club a room upstairs at the Pheasant Inn, Caldewgate, and membership continued to grow throughout the summer until it stood at around 2000.

State Management completely modernised the Pheasant at a cost of £1650 and the Carlisle New Jazz Club opened in December 1963. Club goers were met by bright wallpaper, maizy curtains, a proper bandstand, fitted out with amplifiers and a new bar. The beer pumps were collected from Carlisle Station and fitted only ten minutes before the opening. Members were entertained by local groups such as the Black Tulips Orchestra and a 22-year-old 'tall, well-stacked, glamourous brunette' named Gwynne Challenger of Henderson Road. Gwynne was a music librarian by day and in evening performances her bluesy, rich voice and acute sense of rhythm would 'bring the house down'. Gwynne was asked to join Arthur Curwen's Jazz Trio after he heard her sing in a Carlisle Rag Revue. She became a regular singer at the Pheasant and at Whitehaven Jazz Club.

From January 1964 the Jazz Club above the Pheasant was open just about every evening of the week. There was also an open invitation to 'play it yourself' evenings where, the Kingpin Sextet who would perform in the warm friendly atmosphere of the first floor room of the Kings Head every Monday night would invite members of the audience to contribute to the evening's entertainment by playing a tune they liked on a chosen instrument. Many local musicians visited the club but new faces were always welcome particularly those who did not have the opportunity to play with a group.

Other local pubs also played host to jazz, such as free Sunday lunchtime jazz sessions at the Earl Grey, Botchergate with the Dave Batey-George Mitchellhill duo. One of the highlights of this show being the number, *How High the Moon* featuring George ('Mad Mitch') drumming and wise cracking to the amusement of a highly attentive audience.

There was also the Coach House at Heads Nook, which was the base of the Cumberland Jazz Club. Often there would be impromptu jazz concerts such as Mick Potts and his Gateway Jazz Bands, Jazz Nics or his Railroad Raves. On one occasion the Black Tulips moved from their Head base at the Pheasant to give an informal recital at Carlisle baths.

Inside the Wonder Milk Bar in Devonshire Street.

Jackie Atherton of the Arthur Curwen Trio.

September 1950 and Barney Reay entertains Miss V Foster and Wren M Tagg.

Drummer Brian Rogerson of the Arthur Curwen Trio, January 1963.

The Arthur Curwen Trio playing in the Garrett Club in January 1955. Arthur 'Danny' Curwen is playing the piano.

John and Delcia Ellerton of the King's Head pub who took pity on a bunch of jazz lovers who were looking for a home in 1962 and gave them a room in their pub.

From left, Bill Finlayson of the Downbeat 4, George Baxter and Bill Douglas of the Kingpin Sextet

"DO IT YOURSELF"
JAZZ
SESSIONS
Get " with it " with the
" KINGPINS "
and GUEST ARTISTES
EVERY MONDAY
at 8 p.m. in the
KING'S HEAD
FISHER STREET.
ADMISSION 2/6
Musicans particularly welcome to
" sit in " on these sessions.

THE CARLISLE JAZZ CLUB
"THE PHEASANT INN" — — — — CARLISLE
RESIDENT GROUPS:
THE BLACK TULIPS
THE DOWNBEAT FIVE
TROMBONES INC.
VISITING GROUPS:
The ARTHUR LING QUARTET
JOHN WHITEHEAD TRIO
DAVE FOSTER TRIO
The Committee and members of the Carlisle Jazz Club take this opportunity of expressing their appreciation to the Works Department of the State Management Scheme for their co-operation and help in opening this magnificent Club before the date specified for completion

Gwynne Challenger at Carlisle Jazz Club.

Trombones Incorporated at the King's Head, 1962.

Chris Barber (right) who visited the Cumberland Jazz Club at the Coach and Horses, Heads Nook in 1966.

Miss Britain 1967, Elizabeth Lamb of Morecambe, became the 6000th member of the Carlisle Jazz Club.

Below, a jazz event at Carlisle swimming pool in August 1964 with bass player Derek Hannah of the Black Tulips, who took an unexpected dip with Carlisle Jazz Club members Eric and Margaret Hudson.

A SELECTION OF LOCAL MUSICIANS

Carlisle City Band under its conductor Mr J J Ruddick after they won the Wigton Challenge Cup for the second year running in 1949. Originally the Denton Hill Band, the group was re-formed and re-named in 1946. The band had 30 members and met to rehearse in the Old Mission Hall, Crown Street.

The Bright Lights in the 1950s, Larry Vickers, Frank Logan, Caral Robinson, Dai Watkins and Herbert Vickers who sang harmony and did solo acts with the BATS.

The Mayfair Dance Band pictured in September 1949 after winning the Melody Maker Northumberland Dance Band championship final in Newcastle. From left, Arthur Graham, Jock Hindman, Teddy Nixon, George Foster, George Whitehead, Dave Ruddick, Bob Ruddick, Tommy Walton, Ollie Macaulay, Bill Stephenson and seated, Maurice Sanderson.

Above, right, Teen Combo were popular in the early 1960s and appeared as support band with stars such as Gene Vincent and Sounds Incorporated at the Cosmo. They worked through promoter Duncan McKinnon who ran dances throughout the north. Colin Spark of the Teen Combo went on to form a trio called the Les Taylor Combo, pictured, who played many clubs in The Bright Lights in the 1950s, Larry Vickers, Frank Logan, Caral Robinson, Dai Watkins and Herbert Vickers who sang harmony and did solo acts with the BATS.

Three members of the Gateway Jazz Band, Albert Halliday, Jack Highman and Tennent Brown.

The Danubes at Gretna Hall, Carlisle, in the early 1960s, from left, Duncan McKenzie, Gordon Hind, Alf Ridley, Colin Spark and Gordon Halliwell.

The Danubes in 1962 with Brian Sewell (rhythm), Gordon Hind (drums), Greg 'Alf' Ridley (vocalist), Ron Whittle (lead guitar) and Duncan McKenzie (bass guitar). They were one of Carlisle's early Rock 'n Roll bands playing regularly at the Cameo in the late 1950s. They were paid 10s (50p) a night. Gordon Hind went on to join Four Dollars and Alf Ridley joined the VIPs, Spooky Tooth and Humble Pie. Sadly Duncan McKenzie died in a road accident when he was just 21.

The Terry Savage Trio with Terry Savage (guitar), John McGuiness (drums) and Bobby Goodger (piano). All were former members of the Dave Ruddick Band and were pictured in January 1962 at the Eden and Swiss Court restaurant.

Russell Thomlinson, Ian Barnes, Neil Caddle, Ronnie Swarbrick and Graham Little who were members of the Carlisle rock and roll group Telewele Nothgierc in 1962. Telewele is television in Welsh and Nothgierc is Creighton, their school, spelled backwards!

The Bee Jees a Carlisle group called after a dance of the same name long before the famous Bee Gees. This 1963 photograph shows from left, Brian Cowen, Robert 'Kenny' Kendall, Brian Oliver and Keith Wilkinson. They were all 16 except Kenny who was just 11! The group played at pubs, youth clubs and at the Cameo.

Carlisle group the Brothers Grim in the early 1960s - Eric Freeman (drums), Neil Marshal (vocals), Rod Adams (guitar) and Steve Fearns (vocals and guitar).

Right, The Hotrods pictured at Harraby Youth Centre in 1964. They played at various venues in Carlisle such as the Queen's Hall and the Country Ballroom as well as at youth clubs such as Club 63, Christus Rex and St Margaret Mary's. Phil Bayne played lead guitar, David McRae, rhythm guitar, Walter Jackson, bass guitar and Sinclair Graham, drums.

Below Rue and the Rockets in 1963, from left, Jimmy Slater, Brian Codona, Reuban Slater, Henry Codona and Alan Slater. Photograph courtesy of Brian & Sandra Codona.

RUE & THE ROCKETS
1963
Jimmy Slater, Brian Codona, Reuban Slater, Henry Codona and Alan Slater.

The Richard Dean Sect, a local 1960s band who achieved considerable success both in the Borders and in Germany.

The 22nd Street People in 1966, from left Brian Oliver, lead guitar and vocals, John Coulthard, piano and vocals, Brian Duncan, drums and Neil Marshall, falsetto vocals.

Linda and the Microns from Wigton seen here at the Cosmo in February 1964. From left, John Forster, lead guitar; John Boss, rhythm guitar; Linda, vocals; Alan Lyall, drums and Barry Nixon, bass guitar and vocals. The Microns split up soon afterwards.

The 1967 line up of 22nd Street People - John McVicar, Zeppo Mack, John Coulthard and Brian Oliver.

Pictured above, October 1968 and a new line up for the 22nd Street People - John Coulthard, Brian Oliver, Keith McVicar and John McVicar.

The VIPs, pictured left, who were very popular in the 1960s, back left, Greg 'Alf' Ridley and Jim Henshaw, middle, Walter Johnston and Frank Kenyon and front Mike Harrison. Photograph courtesy of Jim Henshaw.

The 22nd Street People, from left, Brian Oliver, Zeppo Mack, John McVicar and Mike Shannon

November 1971 line up of 22nd Street People, from left, James Wyllie, Brian Oliver and John McVicar and seated, Zeppo Mack.

The Variations were all 16-year-olds from the Northwood Crescent area of the city. Pictured in 1966 they include Ronnie and Raymond Martin, with drummer Roy Batey and vocalist Ian Smith.

Pictured right, Dorothy and Mary Harding who performed at local venues seen here in November 1968.

The Citadel Trio who first played in the Citadel restaurant in July 1968. They were Ron Hodgson, accordion, Alec Slane, bass and Pete Murray on guitar.

In July 1968 Carlisle group Three Good Reasons won a talent competition in Bognor Regis. The band were Michael Maxwell, Gordon Hinds and Chris Nicholson.

The Three Good Reasons became just Two Good Reasons with Chris Nicholson and Michael Maxwell who went on to form Snooty Fox in 1969, along with Charles Cook. All three were former Carlisle Cathedral choristers.

By the early 1970s Chris Nicholson and Michael Maxwell had moved to London, changed their image, and had their first recording on the Colombia Label in August 1971.

The Square Chex consisted of one lad from Lockerbie, two from Kirkpatrick Flemming and two from Carlisle. They included Mike Gillen (vocals) and Ray Parr (guitar). With Rodney Warr as manager they went on to be known as Mythology.

Mythology, formerly the Square Chex.

Mythology changed their name again to Earth and finally became Black Sabbath.

The Black Sabbath story began with a group called the Square Chex, who evolved into Mythology, who evolved into Earth and finally into Black Sabbath which included Birmingham born Ozzy Osbourne and Geezer Butler.

Although Sabbath is best remembered as a heavy metal band in those early days they played the blues. Most of the band lived in a flat on Compton Street, next to Carlisle Technical College. They played several gigs at local village halls, such as Low Hesket and also played at the Cosmo. Black Sabbath left Carlisle for Birmingham in 1969 and the band broke up in the late 1970s.

Black Sabbath

The Runaways, 1969-71, from left, Pete Hoban, Pam and Phil Bayne.

Below, the Pickwick Paupers, a Carlisle group in an old Bentley they used to publicise a folk concert at the Civic Centre. Group members were Jim Atkinson, Dave Blackburn, Charles Leask and John Higgins and the car belonged to Johnny Trantor of Langley Hall.

Above, Skinny Lincoln another popular local band, from left, Pete Arnison (percussion), John Horrocks (alto sax and flute), Peter Gausis (guitar and vocals), Phil McGenn (alto sax and vocals) and Ben Eggleston (bass and vocals).

Photograph courtesy of Olly Alcock.

Below, Universe band members, from left, Olly Alcock, Alan 'Arnie' Armstrong, Box Borrowdale and Mal Thoreburn.

Lemon Grass, from left, David Kent, Stan Morrison, Terry Mills, Gordon Henshaw and front left, Malcolm Mason.

A-Z Carlisle Entertainers

Alf Adamson

Alf Adamson was a musician who enjoyed music for itself and the pleasure it gave to other people. Born in Newcastle, Mr Adamson, began his musical career at the age of eight as a violinist. He went on to be a founder of the Border Square Dance Band, conductor of the Carlisle Light Orchestra and the Carlisle Choral Society Orchestra.

Although his father was a church organist, he taught his son to play the violin and from then there was no stopping Alf. His musical career began in Newcastle cinemas when he used to accompany silent movies, and in his early 20s he became musical director at the Empire, Newcastle.

Then around 1929-30 talking pictures made their appearance putting a lot of musicians out of work, including Alf. He then went to work for the tea merchants, Ringtons and through them he came to Carlisle in 1932. He first worked as a salesman, selling tea around the streets from a horse and carriage and went on to become a manager and retired from the firm in 1968.

In 1941 he joined the forces as a musician with the Royal Marines and was posted to the battleship *Duke of York*. He formed his first orchestra while on board - a twelve piece dance orchestra. While serving with the Royal Marines he served alongside the famous violinist Yehudi Menuhin, whom he greatly admired. Another highlight of life at sea was playing in front of King George VI when he visited the ship.

After four years service, Alf left the forces and formed the six piece Border Square Dance Band in 1951. The band became very popular and was recorded playing in village halls for BBC radio broadcasts. The band made their television debut at the Radio Exhibition at Earls Court, London, which was followed by a children's barn dance which was televised from Manchester. Alf's second Royal entertainment was in Carlisle in 1958 when the Queen visited the city. Alf and his Border Square Dance Band gave an open air performance outside the old Town Hall.

One of his last performances for Royalty was when his band performed for Princess Anne at the Crown & Mitre in April 1972. Alf Adamson and his band finally bowed out after performing at a dinner dance at the Crown and Mitre in February 1973. At the time Alf blamed his retirement on the waning interest in traditional English country music.

By this time he was 72-years-old. He went on to teach violin at several local schools to hundreds of children who fondly remember him to this day. Alf Adamson died in 1985.

Pictured below the Alf Adamson Border Square Dance Band, from left, Bill Stephenson on bass, Gordon Lamb on accordion, Arthur Duckworth on drums, Alf Adamson on violin, Donald Scott

on piano and the sax player's not known.

Olly Alcock

Olly Alcock was born in Huddersfield in 1950. His family moved to Cumbria before he was five, when his father was appointed headmaster at Calthwaite Village School. Olly subsequently went on to attend school at Penrith and then the Carlisle College of Art and Design, Brampton Road. He inherited his love of music from his father.

Olly recalls listening to Radio London and Radio Caroline, who were playing vast amounts of progressive blues. He said, 'I remember revising for exams listening to John Peel on Radio One. He played whole sides of John Mayall's *Bluesbreakers* albums. It was the beginning of guitar heroes, such as Eric Clapton and Peter Green. When Jimi Hendrix came out that was it. That was when I got into Blues. The old adage, 'If you remember the sixties you weren't there' really comes into its own as I try to remember exactly what happened way back when.'

Olly's first band was formed in 1965, consisting of Olly on guitar, Ernie Horn on bass, Graham Luck and Tom Jones (not The Tom Jones) on vocals and Tim Wilson on drums. They called themselves Burgundy

The Burgundy Blues, 1965, pictured outside Graham's house in Blencowe. From left, Olly Alcock (guitar), Tom Jones (vocalist), Tim Wilson (drums), Graham Luck (vocals) and Ernie Horn (bass - which he made himself in the school's woodwork department!)

gigs, with its latter day Cavern atmosphere. It was situated in a nissen hut on a campsite. We also got to play with other bands there, especially Earth, later to become Black Sabbath. Other venues were the Loreburn Hall, Dumfries, Banklands Youth Club, Workington, various village halls like Low Hesket, Ivegill, Welton, Langwathby, Lazonby, Bonds at Cummersdale, the County Hall, Botchergate and, of course, the Cosmo.'

Around 1968 the name Weight was born, originally taken from an old band number that Mike Harrison and Spooky Tooth covered. The Weight ventured into original material and started to build up a small following of people who used to sit cross legged on the dance floors, annoying those who wanted to dance.

Olly Alcock, January 2002, courtesy of News & Star.

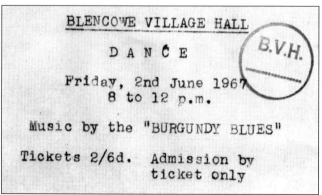

BLENCOWE VILLAGE HALL

D A N C E

B.V.H.

Friday, 2nd June 1967
8 to 12 p.m.

Music by the "BURGUNDY BLUES"

Tickets 2/6d. Admission by
ticket only

The Weight, from left, Olly Alcock, Ernie Horn, Phil Cook, Tom Jones and Ian Borrowdale.

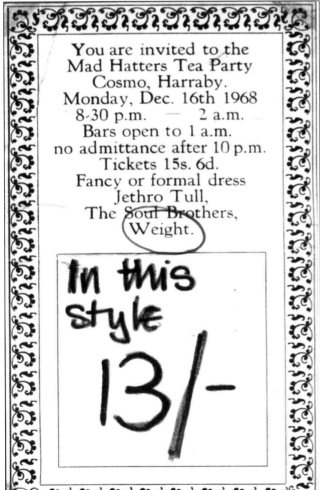

You are invited to the
Mad Hatters Tea Party
Cosmo, Harraby.
Monday, Dec. 16th 1968
8.30 p.m.   ―   2 a.m.
Bars open to 1 a.m.
no admittance after 10 p.m.
Tickets 15s. 6d.
Fancy or formal dress
Jethro Tull,
The Soul Brothers,
Weight.

In this
style
13/-

'Things really started to move in 1969. We were working like beavers to get our equipment up to scratch and we also had a new member in the band - Alan Armstrong took over from Ernie Horn. Now my next big step was to head for London with the band, who were now called Universe. We went to Kingsbury, North London to be precise, renting a house at 110 Dorchester Way.' Olly jokes, 'Surely there will be a blue plaque there by now.'

'Soon we were doing a whole set of self penned numbers, favourites were *The War*, *Gold Watch*, *Threads of Experience*, *Universe* and many others. We used to rehearse with Gerry Rafferty of Baker Street fame. Our first gig in town was supporting Wishbone Ash at the Hampstead Country Club.'

Olly spent the subsequent decade in London with Universe and his later band England. He returned to Cumbria at the end of the seventies after Punk Rock changed the music scene forever. Back in Cumbria he began to teach the guitar. Olly says, 'I started teaching because of Punk. Gigs ceased to exist because Punk took over.'

Today the Olly Alcock Band regularly packs them in at venues both locally and further afield. Olly is now one of the best known figures on the Carlisle music scene.

Universe playing at Reading Festival, 1971. The band was on the bill with Rory Gallagher and Arthur Brown.

Johnny Alone

Johnny Alone was a popular Carlisle singer and impressionist. He was born Johnny Hope in 1939, in Carlisle. After coming out of the RAF in 1963 he formed the Combo '62 Band which played in and around Carlisle until it disbanded in 1966. It was at this time that Johnny changed his name from Hope to Alone and gave up his day job as a sales representative to turn professional.

His father, Bob Hope, manager and organist at Her Majesty's Theatre, maybe inspired his son's talent. Johnny played the guitar-organ in his act and with it could imitate the banjo, trumpet, clarinet, Jew's harp, harmonica and even the bagpipes.

In 1968 his act made national newspaper headlines when a custard pie missed it's target and hit a guest of honour on stage. Luckily the guest saw the funny side of it.

Ronnie Atkinson

Ronnie Atkinson was largely a self-taught musician. He started playing the button accordion when he was only five and soon played it so well his mother bought him a piano accordion. Brought up in Dalston, he came to Carlisle when he was thirteen.

In his younger days he played with the Denton Holme Children's Band and, on one memorable occasion, went to London to play in front of the Queen.

In May 1971 Ronnie bought himself an electric accordion, the only in England at the time. He eagerly awaited its arrival from America. However on playing it, much to his surprise, he heard music and also began to pick up local police communications. On reporting it to the police, it was discovered that the magnetic equipment in the accordion was picking up VHF radio used by the local police.

Ronnie fronted his own band for more than 30 years. They were well known in Cumbria and played at many Masonic functions. Latterly he played the electronic piano accordion and the violin. He died in 1993 at the age of 70.

The Ronnie Atkinson Trio, with Ronnie, unknown and Red Skelton. Red Skelton was also a popular country music entertainer and when he died in the 1990s he was buried wearing his full cowboy costume.

Right, Pam & Phil Bayne.

Pam and Phil Bayne

Pam and Phil Bayne better known locally as the Runaways, both made their debut in the world of music at the tender age of six-years-old. Phil's first public appearance was as a choir boy at St Aiden's Church, Warwick road. Pam's first public appearance was, much to the surprise of her parents, to sing in the Odeon, one of London's largest cinemas during an interval when they asked for volunteers from the audience to come up and sing with the organist. They both attended private schools at the time, Phil at Wykham House, Carlisle and over 300 miles away in London, Pam attended St Helen's School.

In 1963 Hod and the Shakers were formed with Phil (Pip) on guitar/vocals, Kevin Iveson, Selwyn Stubbs, Dave Rutherford and Howard Gaughey. Later in 1964 Phil joined the Hotrods with Dave McRae, Walter Jackson and Sinc Graham performing at, amongst other places, the Queen's Hall, the County and local youth clubs.

Meanwhile Pam's family had moved north to Gretna and Pam, together with a school friend Janet Graham, formed a duo. They both played guitar and sang in harmony in the school choir and at local youth clubs. They were later joined by Janet's sister Francis to become a harmony trio. Their first proper engagement was in Annan when they were invited to appear with Donald Scott and Liz Stewart at one of their performances.

All that was before the Runaways were formed. So how did they meet? Pam heard Phil singing at a youth club organised Folk Music Competition in the Market

The Runaways, from left, Phil and Pam Bayne, Pete Hoban and guest drummer John Goldie from Aspatria.

Hall. Through a mutual friend she contacted Phil and suggested they try out some songs together. At the time he was working for butcher George Cullen in Carlisle and did not turn up for the first arranged meeting - his excuse was that he had been making black puddings all day and was too tired! Still history speaks for itself - Pam or the black puddings?

The Runaways were formed in February 1966. They decided to spend the first year learning new songs with plenty of strong lead and harmony vocals of songs by the Mammas and Papas, Simon and Garfunkel, the Hollies, the Seekers, the Bee Gees, plus oldies by the Everly Brothers, Buddy Holly, Elvis and the Beach Boys. Stage presence, dress and presentation was considered by the pair to be as much part of their act as the music. Pam enjoyed designing and making the stage clothes, re-inventing herself from time to time.

Their involvement in charity work began when they presented a programme of Country and Western num-

bers at a concert held in Her Majesty's Theatre in aid of the Evening News and Star 1967 Christmas appeal.

From the local youth clubs and folk clubs they gradually progressed, building a reputation locally as a harmony duo and by now playing the major clubs and halls in and around Cumbria and south west Scotland. This was followed by an appearance on Border Television's series *One Evening of Late* a folk music half hour produced by Kevin Sheldon. Guest stars appeared each week plus the Pickwick Paupers and Chris Barton who were the resident folk band.

Pam and Phil married in 1968 and a year later they decided to advertise for a third vocalist so that they could concentrate on intricate three part harmony vocals and in 1969 were joined by Pete Hoban.

This proved to be a successful line up and as the local club scene was very busy around that time the trio played regularly three or four nights a week. They also ran a Folk and Country Music Club in Gretna at the Hunters Lodge Hotel, booking guest artistes each week plus audience participation. The Runaways filled in the gaps.

While on holiday in 1971 with both families the trio

Above, Pam and Phil on stage at the London Palladium in February 1975.

Centre, Phil & Pam's trophy for 'services to country music'.

Below, Ali on stage with Pam and Phil.

decided to try their luck at the then prestigious People's National Talent Competition at Butlins, Filey. Up against many hundreds of entries throughout the holiday season they won that round and continued winning through to the semi-finals in Wales narrowly missing a much sought after appearance on the London Palladium for the finals.

By 1973 Pam and Phil who were once again working mainly as a duo were invited by BBC Radio Cumbria to make some recordings which led to many more broadcasts.

Although the duo had always felt more suited to the middle of the road pop chart material, in retrospect it is clear that Country Music was to be where they enjoyed most success. Butlins was now running a National Country Music Competition called Up Country and they won the weekly round at Filey. Following success in further rounds they eventually appeared at the London Palladium in 1975. This led

to appearances on BBC's *Look North* and Border Television this was most definitely a highlight in the duo's career.

Phil's song writing talent was an asset and these songs were included in a recording made by the duo around 1977 by local musician Neil Marshall and sent to a Glasgow record company. On the strength of this Pam and Phil signed a contract with Scottish record company Lismor which led to the release of the LP Border Country in 1978.

Two years later accompanied by other local artistes - Mick Potts and members of his band, together with Bragg the resident band from Carlisle's Working Men's Club, which consisted of Alec Alves, Gordon Hind, Ray Daly and Bob Goodger - they released a successful single about Liverpool FC.

By the 1980s the music scene had started to decline, less pubs/clubs were booking entertainment and it was at this time that Pam and Phil began presenting the *Go Country* music programme on Radio Cumbria. They continued to do so until around 1990 before deciding to call it a day. On the last show, on behalf of the local country music fans, Howard Midgely and Gil Johnston presented them with a trophy for 'Services to Country Music'. It is a much treasured accolade.

They went on to form the Runaways Country Band in 1993 with their daughter Alison (who from the age of five often appeared on stage to sing with her parents), Dave Midgely, Bob Hinkley and Ken Bowman, a line up which lasted two years. Pam and Phil's other two daughters, Kas and Angie, are also both very interested in music and like Ali have always been supportive of their parents.

November 2001 saw Pam and Phil appear at the Sands Centre with other guests including compere Donald Scott, Pete Hoban, Olly Alcock, Trish Clarke, Gentlemen of Jazz and the Salvation Army Band in the' Tribute to New York Appeal Show'.

After 37 years in the business and 35 years of marriage the bond between the two is as strong as ever with local appearances for charity concerts and musically, with the availability of backing tapes, an increased repertoire of songs. Over the years together with Ali many songs have been penned and much time is spent in the studio by Pam and Phil recording them.

In their own words, 'It has been a pleasure working

Cumbria, the North East and south west Scotland's club circuit alongside so many talented musicians and entertainers. Our thanks to the researchers and authors of this publication as we feel very privileged to be invited to share in this, the history of entertainment and entertainers in the area.'

Above, the Runaways in 1980, Pam and Phil with Mick Potts, Bob Goodger, Gordon Hind, Ray Daley, Alec Alves and Sandy Axon, who all accompanied the duo on their Liverpool FC record.

Dave Batey and his Rock 'n Roll Band.

In the mid-fifties a bunch of 15-16 year olds met each week in Carlisle YMCA's attic to play a mixture of traditional and mainstream jazz. At the centre of these enthusiastic budding musicians was Dave Batey, who was trained as a classical pianist, reaching the highest grade possible. The others were Ian Stockdale, later to become city councillor and mayor, John McKie, still successful in the caravan trade, Syd Monk, now a retired police chief superintendent and Tom Lomas, a retired commercial artist and HGV driver.

After a while a new style of music, Skiffle, appeared and, under Dave's guidance, the Zenith Skiffle Group were soon doing the round of youth clubs and church halls. Then another new type of music appeared called rock and roll, which immediately caught the lads' imagination with its vibrant driving beat and the county's first rock and roll band was born.

As bookings poured in, Dave recruited an Elvis look alike Stan Bell as second vocalist and former Terry Degan Skiffle Group guitarist, Kenny Hartness. Local dance bands began recruiting them to play in their intervals and one member can still recall the sight of hundreds of dancers gyrating to the new phenomenon sweeping the world.

Eventually Dave joined the army and after a spell with the Royal Artillery Staff Band, he was selected for Kneller Hall, in the elite Army school of music. He then became principal flute player and piano arranger with the Royal Corps of Signals Staff Band. After twelve and a half year's service Dave stayed in the south, as a pianist for singer David Whitfield then around the cabaret scene, backing artists such as Matt Munro, Dukes and Lee and Ronnie Carroll.

Returning to Cumbria, Dave formed his own big band in the Duke Ellington-Count Basie style. Later Dave returned to the south taking with him that legendary drummer, George Mitchelhill, and talented bass player and vocalist Billy Edmondson.

Eventually the trio returned to their roots, perform-

SUNDAY SCENE
Lunchtime at the Earl of Grey's Place. Dynamic! Dave Batey
With a Cracking New Percussionist & Special Guest
12 to 2 — ADMISSION 2/-
Within easy lurching distance of Town Centre
THE EARL GREY INN

ing in clubs and other venues, before Dave fell ill with cancer. It was during this trying time that he met West Cumbrian lass Isabel, who became his wife. After numerous operations Dave appeared on the music scene again, bravely ignoring his condition arranging music for big bands such as the Horace Stone Orchestra, based in London, and Carlisle's Cliff Elland Band.

In 1997 former members of Dave Batey's Rock and Roll Band staged a benefit show at Harraby Catholic Club where a huge crowd gathered to be entertained by music from Sounds of Swing, Ken Hillary's Disco and a comedy slot by 'Mad Mitch' (George Mitchelhill). They performed in honour of Dave, who was sent home to Whitehaven in a limo with the proceeds.

The Dave Batey Rock and Roll Band, on stage at the Lonsdale, Carlisle, about 1957. From left, Kenny Hartness, Stan Bell, Dave Batey, Tommy Lomas, John McKie and Syd Monk.

Robert 'Bonzo' Burns

Robert 'Bonzo' Burns was born in Newcastle. He left the city at the age of eleven as an evacuee during the war. Bonzo's recollections appeared in the *Evening News & Star* in June 1969. He said, 'I remember the train journey to Carlisle and seeing real live cows in green fields, and apples on trees. I had never seen that before. I went to two schools in Carlisle, first St Patrick's then Grosvenor College. I joined the army at 17, in my father's old regiment, the Royal Northumberland Fusiliers. I got myself shot in the forearm on a rifle range in 1945. I was waving a white flag at the time to signal inspecting targets. I did all sorts of jobs after I left the army - milkman, salesman, debt collector and newspaper deliveries...'

Bonzo was also one of the Cameo's most famous doormen. He eventually became a barman with the State Management and got his first pub, the Nelson Bridge, very quickly. He will be remembered most for his years as licensee of the Cumberland Wrestlers Pub between 1964 and 1984. Bonzo was never on stage but he was one of Carlisle's colourful characters and as such almost qualifies as an entertainer!

The late Robert 'Bonzo' Burns, manager of the Cumberland Wrestlers in Currock Street during the Carlisle State Management Scheme.

Billy Bowman Band

The Billy Bowman Band, founded in Cockermouth around 1916, was one of the more popular country bands, and with 87 years history of entertaining Cumbrians is certainly the longest surviving. The band passed from to father to son. Billy Bowman junior retired on Millennium New Years Eve after more than 50 years playing himself.

'The term country band is not to mean Country and Western, rather playing in the country,' says Billy Junior, he continues, 'There are not many village fairs, farmers' or hunt balls or young farmers' dos the band didn't play for at one time or another.'

Billy junior's grandfather, Johnny also played concertina and banjo in a Broughton Carnival Band.

Great Broughton Carnival Band in the 1920s. Billy Bowman junior's grandfather Johnny is in the centre with the banjo.

A family affair, the band was formed by Billy Bowman senior who played the melodian, later transferring to the accordion, quickly followed by his sister Florrie, aged 13 on the piano, whom Billy had encouraged. They were joined by another brother Jack on the fiddle. The band were never short of engagements and indeed played at the opening of several village halls in the county. Billy recalls one in particular being Braithwaite Institute, which celebrated their 70th anniversary in 1997 with Billy junior playing. His father and Florrie had played at the opening. The occasion was made unique when Billy took Auntie Florrie along aged 92 - she 'did a spot' 70 years after opening the place.

Billy junior was going out playing with the band as early as 1949/50 when aged just 12 or 13 whilst still at school. He recalls, 'They needed a drummer and so I was put onto drums, however I went in the Navy from 1954 to 1956, naturally I played with the ship's dance band. When I finished my service I went to work for two years but came back to join the band.'

Quite often the band appeared in Carlisle, in venues

such as the Silver Grill, Cosmo and the Crown and Mitre, usually for country associated groups such as the young farmers, pony clubs and weddings.

Billy Junior remembers a conversation with brilliant Carlisle drummer George 'Mad Mitch' Mitchelhill. George recalled playing with the Edenaires Big Band when they shared the stage at the Carlisle Show dance with the Billy Bowman Band in the Market Hall. 'We played for a solid hour and not a soul got up to dance, the minute you lot came on everybody was up dancing,' Mitch had said.

But as Billy says, 'No disrespect to the Edenaires, who were a superb band, it was a matter of horses for

courses. Being an agricultural show, the dancers, all country folk were more used to whooping it up to a Canadian Three step than smooching to a slow fox-trot.'

During the 60 s after Billy Junior had taken over, pop groups were becoming popular. A lot of the older bands fell by the wayside, so the fiddle was replaced with a guitar. The guitarist being Florrie's son John, making it even more of a family affair.

Some years later Billy junior joined guitarist James Garner, appearing at many clubs in Carlisle as the comedy duo act Double Trouble. Billy was the stand up comedy half and he would do Frank Spencer, a vicar or sometimes dressed in Benny Hill style in army gear when he would appear during the act from the main entrance blowing a bugle. This backfired somewhat one summer's night when they first appeared at the Garlands Hospital Social Club, when Billy made his way to the front door only to find it locked. As he says, 'I can tell you it's not funny standing in army gear with a bugle in your hand in the middle of a mental hospital.'

Top, entertaining in the vicarage garden, Cockermouth, 1925. From left, Florrie on the piano, the banjo player is unknown, Billy senior with sax and accordion, Billy Rook on trumpet and Annie Watson on drums.

Above, Billy Bowman jnr in his shop in Lowther Went, Cockermouth.

THE FELL & MOORLAND WORKING TERRIER CLUB

"TERRIER NIGHT"

Dinner Dance Social

in the

CUMBRIA BALLROOM, WORKINGTON

on SATURDAY, 28th FEBRUARY, 1976 at 7 p.m.

Music by BILLY BOWMAN

Lucky N⁰ 177   Tickets £2·30 each

A barn dance at Bothel in the 1960s, Alf Stephenson on sax, Robert McHendry on trumpet, Billy Bowman Snr with fag and accordion, Florrie on piano and Billy Jnr on drums.

These days Billy Jnr. still plays the baritone sax with Music Masters, a Whitehaven Big Band and drums with Dearham Brass Band. He told me, 'It was always my ambition to have a music shop. In my mind I wanted a shop to replace the void left by Jimmy Dias' old place in Botchergate, Carlisle, where my father and I had bought most of our instruments.

'I like to feel that like Jimmy we have a proper music shop selling brass and woodwind, in fact all instruments not just guitars and keyboards. I also teach one or two youngsters, that gives me a lot of pleasure. I am very lucky to be doing what I do, being involved with music all my life and having the support of my wife Margaret for 43 years.'

Billy said that William, one of his grand children is already showing a talent for music so hopefully he will carry on the family tradition.

The Cave Dwellers

The Cave Dwellers was the idea of Tom Foster who wanted to form a rock group. So, early in 1964, the new 'Border sound' emerged on the pop music scene. At the time people said Border sound might displace the Merseybeat as the ultimate development of a group with three guitars. Inspired by Little Richard and by Sounds Inc., the Cave Dwellers decided to refresh Carlisle pop which they thought was a bit behind the times.

The Cave Dwellers were the first beat band in Carlisle to incorporate saxophones, along with guitars, piano and drums. With this mix they broke away from conventional pop, while keeping up with the latest trends. Their style was based on rhythm and blues, but they played everything from jazz to rock.

All the players were from Carlisle. John McGaughlin, lead guitarist was previously with the Four Dollars. Drummer Brian Rogerson was once in the Dollars line up and the two sax players, Tom Foster and Bill Finlayson, were experienced as was Pete Batey on bass guitar and Richard Atkinson as vocalist. Tom Foster had played with the Bullets, a London band and Bill Finlayson was previously a member of the Downbeat Five.

At a gig in the County Ballroom they were given an enthusiastic welcome with girls crowding round the stage screaming and yelling to them. The girls wanted autographs which was unheard of in Carlisle at that time.

In January 1965 the group split up but they were back together by July, stronger than ever when they gave a performance at the Market Hall.

They became resident band at the Sunday night 'stomp ins' at the Cosmo where their first appearance was so successful that it gained them summer bookings at places as far afield as Darlington, Stockton, York, Scarborough, Glasgow and Edinburgh. Locally they gained a fan club of hundreds, who wore metal badges painted blue to match their jackets with Cave Dwellers printed in red letters around the edges.

After losing their drummer Brian Rogerson, who went to Germany, and being unable to find a replacement the Cave Dwellers finally split for good.

The Cave Dwellers in the 1960s, from left back, Dave Foster, Gordon Hind, Howard Sims. Front, Tom Foster, Derek Brown and Bill Finlayson.

Arthur 'Danny' Curwen

Arthur 'Danny' Curwen was greatly respected by all musicians yet he was a self-taught pianist who could not read music.

He was born in 1931 in Denton Holme, and became a plumber with Frederick Batey. He fought in Korea in the early 50s during his national service. After he was demobbed the Arthur Curwen Trio became a popular feature at the city's Carrow House Hotel, Carleton. He first had George 'Mad Mitch' Mitchellhill and then Brian Rogerson on drums, with Jimmy Oliver on bass with Jackie Atherton as the vocalist.

Arthur was also a founder member of the Jazz Club at the Pheasant, Caldewgate, Carlisle. He moved to Cornwall in the early 60s where he became a full-time musician. There he played with stars like Freddie Starr, Kenny Baker and Gerry Stevens.

He returned to Carlisle in the early 80s, at which time he became a foreman on a government scheme and his trio was a regular musical feature all over the city, mostly playing for charity. In this period Arthur and Brian Rogerson were joined first by Bill Edmondson and then Dave Rutherford on bass with Ronnie Walker providing the vocals.

Arthur also played with leading musicians like Mick Potts, Billy Douglas and Tony Tears. Towards the end Arthur's hands were affected by arthritis but he never let it affect his playing.

After his death in February 1992 at the age of 61, Arthur was given a traditional jazz man's funeral, as he had wanted. Mick Potts led a ten piece band, an augmented version of his Gateway outfit at Carlisle Crematorium. They played the New Orleans funeral number, *Just Walk With Thee* before and after the service first as a march and then as a stomp.

His close friend and colleague Brian Rogerson recalls, 'Arthur had the ability to be an international star, but was happy playing anywhere and he did not seek fame. He was held in enormous respect. Arthur's music was a mixture of Oscar Peterson and Errol Garner, two pianists he loved to listen to, yet with his own style. He was a drummer's dream to play with.'

Local musicians playing at Carlisle Crematorium for the funeral of Arthur Curwen.

Brian Davis

Brian Davis served an apprenticeship in engineering with Pratchett Bros (Mitchells) of Denton Holme in the late 1950s and early 1960s. While doing his training he was able to build a reputation as a singer and entertainer. He was blessed with a great voice and was associated with some of Carlisle's best known musicians. Brian also won some prestigious talent competitions. He still lives in Carlisle and often entertains at charitable functions.

Some of the finalists in a 'Find the Singer' contest held in the Cameo Ballroom in April 1961. The winner was Brian McTaggart (Davis) who is seated second from right. Also on the picture, seated left, is Johnny Alone and leaning over is second place man Pete Hoban.

Geoff Dickens

Geoff Dickens enjoyed music from a young age taking parts in various school choirs, as a boy soprano and in a school production of *H.M.S. Pinafore*. He became involved in more stage work at an early age and was part of a concert in the City Hall with the local Music Society and various other local artists. (This venue was to be used after the demise of Her Majesty's Theatre.) This was not the best of starts in show business.

Geoff said, 'I performed as a duet with another soprano, Dick Bell, but we forgot the words. I did better on my next venture, singing and story telling on the radio programme *Bill Cain's Country Dance*.

'After my school years, as a teenager, like most, I was influenced by early Skiffle, country music and Elvis. I entered various song contests, won some and lost some. My most enjoyable was when I won at Butlins, Ayr, singing *If I were a Rich Man* from *Fiddler on the Roof*.

"I went on to gain experience with a little help from my friends, by touring all the local sing-a-long venues and working the club circuit using some arrangements by Dave Batey. You needed 'dots' (sheet music) as each club had its own resident band which would play for your spot. At the Ex-Servicemen's Club I was

Below HMS Pinafore performed by the Robert Ferguson school in April 1954. Geoff is the small boy in the middle of the front row.

greatly influenced and encouraged by Lance Armstrong with Ray Purves and Gordon Halliwell. Other locals who I would say influenced me were Maurice Petry and Tom Lomas, who are still great friends of mine today.

'I became resident compere at the Royal Oak, Sour Nook, Sebergham. I also performed duo work with Dennis Watt (bass guitarist) who used to play with the Dolls. We called ourselves the Odd Balls. Around this time I decided to play the guitar in my act, this enabled me to perform more country songs and opened up more venues on the country pub circuit to me. Being a late starter on the guitar I needed some help, which was provided by Peter McCaffery, who 30 years on is still trying to make a guitarist out of me.

'I then played with the Thwaites Family (two generations.) but mostly worked with Dennis Westmorland in the Country Rovers performing at hunt balls and barn dances. Sometimes we were joined at the larger gigs by Tony Renney, who would also help with my guitar tuition.

'I also sang in the chorus of the Carlisle Choral Society, which was very enjoyable, performing in Gilbert and Sullivan's *HMS Pinafore*, the *Mikado* and *Iolanthe*.

'In May 1984 I sang in the home of country music itself, Nashville, Tennessee. I have also performed on the Carlisle Great Fair Stage with various local musicians, such as Dennis Watt, Bob Hinkly and Tony Renney.

'I have two CDs to my credit and some radio and TV work, having being featured on Border TV's *Out from the Crowd*. I am still working as a single act or duo performing 50s/60s standards and country music.

'I consider myself fortunate to have been able to sing and entertain for the past 40 years plus. I have enjoyed all the venues and making a lot of friends along the way. I still get a buzz when I pack my gear up and go on the road again to another gig.

'Assisting Marie with this book has enabled me to meet many old friends and colleagues, who I have known and worked with over the years. We have enjoyed chatting, reminiscing and bringing their memories and photographs together for publication.'

Geoff Dickens on stage at Butlins, Ayr, 1984.

Below, Geoff in the Mikado, pictured bottom left.

The Edenaires

The Edenaires were also known as the Redcoats and played regularly on the Duncan McKinnon circuit which included Border dances at the Market Hall, playing opposite stars such as Acker Bilk.

They were extremely popular north of the Border where they would do a yearly tour of Scotland. They regularly filled two double decker buses with fans who would travel from Carlisle to Dumfries Drill Hall for the Saturday night dances where the huge hall would be packed. Rumour has it that these dances always finished early due to the law about no dance continuing into the Sabbath, (and not because of the fights which were always breaking out in the crowd!)

They also played regularly for a decade at the Coach House with Mick Potts on Sunday nights.

Cliff Eland's Big Band

Cliff Eland's Big Band played an important part in the Carlisle entertainment scene for a very long time, although it only came into being in 1980. Its founder Cliff Eland was making music long before that. He had played in many local bands since the late 1940s, mainly on accordion, but his secret ambition was to have his own band.

Cliff Eland's first band was the Selmar Dance Band, which had two accordionists, a drummer and a pianist. It was 1942, Cliff was fifteen and had just moved to Carlisle from Aspatria. The band's debut was at St Aiden's Church, Warwick Road, with Cliff on accordion. He had bought the instrument for £5 at the age of thirteen. A few years later he changed to saxophone.

Cliff Eland playing a solo with his band in the 1960s at the Crown and Mitre.

By day Cliff was a paint sprayer at James Bendall and later a tool maker at Metal Box. During the war years Cliff's group was the house band at the Cameo Ballroom, Botchergate. The eight piece band staying there for eleven years.

During the war Cliff met his wife whilst she was singing for troops at the John Peel Hut, where the

Cliff leads his band in the early 1990s

Civic Centre is today. The Woolpack, Milbourne Street, was also a regular venue. The band could also be seen at charity functions, social clubs, ballrooms and private parties.

Cliff would dress in black evening suit and bow tie, all the others wore white shirts, black trousers, red ties but no jackets.

Cliff combined a career as a musician with that of a

highly successful business man. He ran the Aero Precision Factory in Carlisle for 22 years before selling up in 1991. He developed the business from a tiny workshop to a company employing 40 people with a multi-million pound turnover.

However it was as leader of the Cliff Eland Big Band, which he established in 1980, that he was best known to most people. Cliff continued to play right to the end which came on 22 January 1995 when he was aged 68 years.

Since his death, a group of members have worked to keep the band and Cliff's memory alive. Cliff Atwood, a veteran of other Carlisle bands looks after the music, whilst vocalist Pete Hoban has become 'the booker' and keeps the engagement book full. The style of music played has not changed since its inception, but it is brought up to date as tastes in music have varied. If you still get nostalgic about the days of the big bands, you will certainly enjoy listening to the Cliff Eland Big Band of today.

Bill Finlayson

Bill Finlayson became interested in jazz as a teenager having been influenced by Benny Goodman. When he was fourteen his father gave him a clarinet and he began to take lessons. After several weeks his teacher told him not to come back as he said Bill wasn't practising enough. Bill went home and practised and after only a week his teacher was amazed at the improvement.

In 1957 Bill began work as an apprentice hairdresser. For the next year all his spare time was devoted to practising his music - on his Thursday half-day off and at the weekends. Even Saturday nights when all his friends were out on the town, Bill stayed at home to practise and didn't go out for a year.

Bill joined his first band in 1958, playing traditional jazz with Peter Lince on trumpet, Harry Roberts on piano, Sycamore Smith on bass, George Robinson on banjo and John on trombone. They were called the Jazz Cardinals and they took part in the 'Top Town Competition' at Manchester.

In 1959 Bill moved into mainstream jazz and joined the Gateway Jazz Band. He played with them for two years.

On Thursday afternoons Bill would go along to the Garrett Club in Devonshire Street where he met Dave

Bill Finlayson rehearsing for the 'Top Town' show in 1959. Photograph courtesy of the Carlisle Journal.

Jock Hymen, Bill Finlayson and Dave Batey.

107

Foster. Dave wanted to form a modern jazz group and so the Downbeat Five (sometimes four) came about. The new band had Dickie MacGrath on trumpet, Dave Foster on piano, Brian Rogerson on drums, Ron 'Benny' Oosthuizen on double bass and Bill on tenor sax.

At this time Border Television sound engineers would also meet at the Garrett. The liked modern jazz and invited the Downbeat Five along to the studios one Sunday morning to make an audio tape. Bill recalls,

'That would have been in 1963 when we also played at the Cleathorpes Jazz Festival.'

At the same time as playing with the Downbeat Five, Bill also played in Jock Hymens' big band the Sessionaires, often playing at the County, Botchergate.

However by now the popularity of big bands was beginning to fade, so Tom Foster, Dave Foster's 21-year-old cousin, suggested forming a rock band, and thus the new 'Border Sound' emerged on the pop music scene in the form of the Cave Dwellers. After the Cave Dwellers disbanded in the mid 1960s Bill went on to join a band with Ray Parr, called Jawbone, the name being derived from a Bob Dylan number. He remained with them for three years.

Bill gave up playing in 1972 and did not start again until around 1986 at which time he joined a jazz funk band Complexion playing tenor and alto sax alongside Brian Melville on keyboard, Brian Rogerson on drums and Billy Edmondson on bass. They would regularly play at the Shambles, now Finnegans Wake, Lowther Street, and the Waterloo on the A69, on Sunday lunchtimes. They were also popular on Thursday nights at the London Road Tavern. Complexion disbanded in 1987, at which time Bill gave up playing. Today Bill continues to run his hair salon in Corporation Road.

GENTLEMEN! — THERE'S A VACANT
CHAIR FOR YOU AT . . .
APPOINTMENTS ONLY . . .   NO WAITING
11 Victoria Place, Carlisle

BILL FINLAYSON'S
Gentlemen's Hair Stylist
BOOK YOURS NOW!
Telephone 28642

Photographs, from top, Bill Finlayson, Peter Lince and John ?

Bill Finlayson's hairdressing shop, May 1966.

Jawbone, August 1971, from left, Philip Logan, Ray Parr, Bill Finlayson and Tony Hill.

108

Tom Foster

In February 1948, at the age of only 35, Tom Foster celebrated 21 years as a band leader. Speaking to the *Carlisle Journal* at the time, Mr Foster said he thought this was a record, certainly locally.

A native of Carlisle, and a great admirer of the American sax player, Tommy Hodges, Tom started to learn the violin when he was only seven-years-old. He became a conductor when he was just fourteen. The band he conducted was a family affair, and consisted of his father and himself as violinists, with his brother and sister as pianists.

The quartet played at village halls in the district. Later his father took up the banjo, which at the time was a popular instrument. Tom in turn learned to play the saxophone and the clarinet, and his brother the accordion.

The band developed until, in 1934, it was playing regularly at the Queens Hall, the Viaduct, with three saxophonists, two trumpeters, a bass, piano, drums and a vocalist. Tom's brother took over the conductorship when Tom left Carlisle for business reasons, later returning to the city in 1940.

During the war the band performed almost every night at military camps in the area. After the Queens Hall was de-requisitioned in October 1946, Tom Foster and his colleagues played there three nights a week.
Tom Foster's 'coming of age' was celebrated at the Queen's Hall, by over 350 people. Two other local bands, led by Cyril Lowes and the Irving brothers showed their regard for Tom by playing. It was a much appreciated gesture of friendship. During the evening there was also a cabaret performance by local artistes. Tom continued to lead his band through the next decade.

Pictured, Tom Foster, celebrating 21 years as a conductor.

Tommy Giacopazzi

Tommy Giacopazzi was inspired by Elvis Presley at an early age. Tommy is now aged 63 and has had a virtual non-stop entertainment career of more than 50 years.

His career began at the age of six, when he became involved in St Bede's Junior School Christmas concerts which he continued to be involved in until he left at the age of eleven to attend St Patrick's Secondary School. Here from the ages of twelve to fourteen, encouraged by his school friend Tom Lomas, he joined the Border Regiment Cadets and played side drum in the Marching Bugle Band.

When he was fifteen he went to work at Todd's Wool Factory, alongside Mick Potts, before joining the Gas Board where, from the age of 21, he was employed as a gas fitter for thirty years.

In the days of the Eden Youth club, in the mid-1950s, Tommy joined the Dave Batey Band at the age of sixteen to play drums and sing rock 'n roll songs. He played with the band for about a year and then had a quiet spell where he sang occasionally in the local clubs, just for the fun of it.

In May 1963 at the age of 23 Tommy took to the stage at the County Ballroom, Botchergate to battle for top honours in the Carlisle Teen and Twenty Club's 'Find the Singer' competition. With a swinging version of Bobby Darin's *Clementine* he sang himself to a win of a £5 cheque and an audition with Columbia Records.

The following year Tommy bought his first drum kit for £13 and formed a trio with various bass players. They worked all the clubs in Carlisle and West Cumbria as the Pazzi Trio and did well through the 1960s.

From 1967 as a member of the BATS he became involved in charity functions, having performed at 1000s over the years. Tommy remembered playing, 'From the days of the freezing cold conditions of the old Market Hall to more recent functions held in the comfort of the Sands Centre.'

With the end of the Pazzi Trio in the late 1960s he joined up with Rich Jefferson, who played the piano, doing jobs as a duo for a while before being joined by Brian Witherington, a guitar vocalist and Howard Midgley, a bass player. They played through the early 1970s as the Brian Rich Four. Tommy recalls, 'We had some marvellous, great nights. Then in the late seventies we packed up but I continued as a trio with Howard and his son Dave Midgley, playing as Phase Three until the early eighties, doing the local clubs and the Lido, Silloth. Even doing a short spell as the Gillbillies fronted by Gill Johnston, which was great fun.'

Front left, Tommy Giacopazzi, aged seven or eight, taking part in one of the St Bede's School concerts.

From about 1983 Tommy was joined by Dave Rutherford and Brian Dunk, playing as the Tommy Pazzi Band until sadly, in 1986, Dave died. Tommy recalls, 'I felt then more than ever it was time to call it a day. Yet after a while I got interested in some modern backing technology and formed Topaz in 1997. As

The Marching Bugle Band.

May 1963 and Tommy wins the Carlisle Teen and Twenty Club's 'Find the Singer' competition.

Today's Topaz, Ronnie Walker and Tommy Giacopazzi.

a duo with Ronnie Walker, a longstanding friend, we are enjoying entertaining people in the clubs and hotels in and around Carlisle and West Cumbria, with the odd function further a field. I never thought I would still be involved in entertainment after all this time, but basically I suppose I am just lucky. Looking back there's been a lot of great nights with some great pals.'

Bill Gore

Bill Gore entertained in Carlisle during the 1950s and 60s, performing his novelty clog act at Her Majesty's Theatre and other local clubs. His act included a 26" long clog, which Bill claimed was the biggest clog in the world.

In January 1970, Bill was scheduled to appear for a week in cabaret at the Selby Forks Motel on the A1. Then he found out that he was needed for a television appearance on Hughie Green's *Opportunity Knocks* show. To Bill's amazement, the motel manager, Mr Harvey Bash, promptly cancelled the cabaret show until Bill was available again for the Saturday night show.

Mr. Bill Gore

Pictured opposite, Lemongrass outside Carlisle Castle just prior to touring Germany in 1975, from left, Gordon Henshaw, Terry Mills, Ann Robertson, Geoff Morris and Malcolm Mason.

Gordon Henshaw

Drummer Gordon Henshaw remembers his early years when he lived at the Gretna, Lowther Street when it was run by his parents for a time before his father's death in 1962.

'Entertainment was provided by the likes of Alf Adamson and his band or Dave Ruddick's band. I also recall the great Scottish comedian Dave Willis would call in to do a turn on the occasions when he was in Carlisle to appear at Her Majesty's Theatre.

'My mother tells me that in the early 1960s the Gretna was one of the first venues to hold regular bingo sessions at which Gladys Hogarth would play the organ in the intervals. Some of the money raised on these nights would be donated to the Lowther Street Congregational Church, which was next door. I think this was to appease them because of the noise levels.'

Being the younger brother by eleven years to veteran rocker Jim Henshaw of VIPs fame Gordon said, 'There was always music in the home. I was firstly influenced by the likes of Chuck Berry and the Beatles before my interests changed to the sounds of US soul, southern rock music and in particular Van Morrison and the Average White Band.'

Although Gordon was largely self taught to play the drums, he did take some early lessons from George 'Mad Mitch' Mitchellhill.

Gordon joined Rob Lowther, Brian Lorimer, John Ellwood and Dave Kent collectively known as Badge, his first band in 1970. He remembers playing the Hilltop as support band for the Bay City Rollers. Gordon laughs as he tells me, 'We once even had a police escort out of Dumfries after the crowd tried to attack us.

'I joined Lemongrass in 1973, replacing Walter Johnston. We played locally but also felt the need to move on so we began to work over in the North East, Sunderland way. In 1975 we toured Germany for three months, playing at US Army bases. For this tour we had taken on a girl singer.'

Gordon left Lemongrass in 1977 and went on to work for a year with local band Felix, which included Billy Simpson, Neil Marshall, Mike Gillen and Scott Morris.

Hesket and District Young Farmers

Annual Dinner Dance

at NEWBY GRANGE HOTEL
on Thursday, 15th December. 1983
7.30 for 8.00 p.m.
Dancing to **COUNTRY ROVERS**
Tickets £6.50 each

There then followed a two year stint with another popular local band Captain Flint with his brother Jim, Brian Dunk, Phil Brown and Phil Logan. Gordon said Phil Logan was one of the best all round musicians he played with. The band also played the Cosmo with Captain Flint supporting the Glitter Band, though Gary Glitter was not there.

From 1980 to 1986 Gordon became part of Dennis Westmorland's Country Rovers, taking four years off before rejoining them from 1996 to 2000.

He said, 'I have now sold my drums, however I sometimes strum the guitar. These days I prefer to fit in a game of golf in between working for Cumbrian Newspapers.' However Gordon and Susan's teenage children Andrew and Lyndsey have plans of their own to work in the entertainment business. Having taken part in Green Room Theatre pantomimes and Carlisle Musical Society productions at the Sands Centre, Andrew hopes to become an actor and Lyndsey plans a career as a dancer/singer.

Ian 'Sherb' Herbert

Ian 'Sherb' Herbert, was first influenced by popular music in 1960 when he was eleven and heard the Shadows. Then at the age of fourteen he met and began carrying gear for Hod and the Shakers, namely Howard Gaughey, Ces Stubbs, Kevin Iverson and Dave Rutherford before joining them in 1963. The following year the group changed their name to Rivals.

They played various gigs around the county using Andy Park as their agent when he lived at Rockcliffe. However tragedy struck in 1966 when the band's vehicle collided with a tree at the Friends School, Wigton whilst travelling home from a gig, resulting in the death of Howard which hit everyone very badly.

In 1967 Ian formed a band called the Word with Sinclair Graham, Alan Hill and Kevin Iverson, a former member of Hod and the Shakers.

In 1969 Ian along with Pete Batey, Kevin Iverson and Frank Kenyon formed Jam Swamp which changed its name in 1970 to Timothy Pink before finally becoming known as Junkyard Angel. Ian recalls, 'We played regularly with Black Sabbath around Cumbria and the south of Scotland. We also played the Tow Bar, Egremont with Status Quo.'

In 1971 Carlisle born Mike Harrison returned to the city and work began on an album backed by Junkyard Angel resulting in an LP entitled 'Mike Harrison' which was recorded at the Island Studios, London. In October 1971 the *Evening News and Star* reported, 'The LP is the outstanding waxing among Island Records latest batch of releases - in fact along side Cat Stevens' *The Teaser and the Firecat*, it could be the

Pictured at the Pheasant pub in Carlisle in the 60s are Ian Herbert, George Mitchelhill, Rob Holliday (standing) and Ian Alecock. Ian formed the group Junkyard Angel while Ian Alecock and George Mitchellhill toured the clubs for six years as Mel and Mitch, and Rob formed the Dolls, which later became the Voltaires.

Junkyard Angel

year's best collection from that label.'

Junkyard Angel went on to plan and record their own album however due to problems with politics and finance this was never released. Ian said that he still has a tape recording of it. 'We played the university circuit and did two German tours with Mike Harrison singing.' recalls Ian, 'We also backed Free on an English tour.'

In 1973 Ian worked in the studios at Island records for about 18 months during which time he worked with Bob Marley amongst other Jamaican acts, on an album called *Soul of Jamaica*, which he does not have a copy of but would dearly love to get hold of. Junkyard Angel disbanded in 1975.

Pete Hoban

Pete Hoban has some 40 years experience as a singer with a wide repertoire. As a novice feeling his way in the 60s he started in the clubs as a guitar playing vocalist. In the 1970s he was a compere and then moved into the cabaret scene before joining the Cliff Eland Big Band in the 1980s, also taking part in Carlisle Musical Society's production of *Calamity Jane* in 1987.

Pete said that he has always had a keen interest in music, influenced by Elvis Presley in particular. At the age of sixteen he received his first guitar, a gift from his brother, on his return from service in Italy in 1956.

Sixteen-year-old Pete Hoban remembers entertaining passengers on a train to Newcastle.

In the mid1950s 'skiffle' was THE thing so he and a group of friends followed the growing trend and formed a skiffle group, calling themselves The Teenagers. Pete laughs, 'We only played two gigs at the Eden Youth Centre in the old NAAFI Club. After the second performance when our tea chest and broom handle bass player fell over, too drunk to stand up we never got asked back.'

Not to be daunted by this early disappointment in his career, his next move was to take part in a television

'Find the Singer' contest held at the Cameo, Botchergate, in April 1961. Pete sang Elvis' hit *I can't help falling in love with you* and took second place to his old school friend Brian (Davis) McTagart. This success got him noticed on the scene.

Around this time he began to take an interest in the big bands, often going along to the Crown and Mitre to hear Bobby Laing and the Mayfair Dance Band perform. When the opportunity arose to sing with Cliff Eland's early eight piece band for a year, he took it. By day he worked as a GPO engineer and by night performed with the band in the same style as his heroes of swing such as Frank Sinatra, Tony Bennett and Nat King Cole.

His next move was to make three appearances on Border TV's *Music Makers* for which he was paid the princely sum of £8 for his first show and £12 for the next two. This led to an invitation to appear on Hughie Green's Roadshow at Whitehaven's Civic Hall in 1967, at which other local musicians such as Bill Gore were also making an appearance.

In 1969 Pete answered an advert for a third person to join a trio. After a meeting at the local Wimpy Burger Bar in the Crescent, with Pam and Phil Bayne he joined the Runaways. For three years he formed the third link in the three part set up of this popular act on the Cumberland club scene. He recalls winning a heat of a national talent contest at Butlins Filey holiday camp in 1971.

Pete laughs as he recalls another talent contest which he entered at the Kirklinton Hall Border Club in the 1960s, where he would often sing with the resident bands. The first prize was the chance to cut a record,

2nd prize was £14 and 3rd prize was £8. Pete said, 'I don't recall who won but I came second and a policeman took third place. A few weeks had passed and none of us had received our prizes, so we went along with this policeman to enquire with Bill Cain as to what had happened. He eventually grudgingly paid up but the winner never got to make his record.'

In 1973 Pete moved on, firstly working as compere at Wigton British Legion as a warm up act and singing with the resident band the Dick Barton Trio. He went on to work with many other local acts including the Arthur Curwen Quartet, the Pazzi Trio, Jazzer Boyle and also Billy Nobel and the Lance Armstrong Trio of the United Services Club. As a solo vocalist and guitarist on the club scene with arrangements by Dave Batey, he performed locally at Brampton, Gilsland and West Cumberland venues as well as further afield at Carnforth, Lancaster, and in the North East.

After joining the BATS in the 1970s he became involved in a lot of their charity work. Taking his turn as last of the King Bats in 1981/82. As with many other local entertainers his involvement in charity work did not end with the demise of the BATS. For the last 20 years he has worked to raise money for the Stroke Club and with the Cliff Eland Big Band has raised money for Eden Valley Hospice.

In the 1980s Pete moved into the cabaret scene at which time he sang as part of nationwide tours with bill-toppers such as Ken Dodd, Les Dennis and Jim Bowen and the Comedians. He counts this time as one of the highlights of his career.

At this time he was involved in doing supporting jobs for Border Entertainments. One of these jobs was at Blackpool where he would provide the early evening entertainment at the Ivy Leaf Club and the late night spot at the Beach Comber Night Club. 'It was hard work, especially as I had to travel home for work the next day,' recalls Pete, 'I entered another talent contest whilst there. I didn't win but I gained some

Peter Hoban with Pam and Phil Bayne as the Runaways, after their win at Filey in the early 1970s

Top right, an advert for Pete Hoban to sing at Dalston Hall, where he would perform popular music with some country and western numbers.

DALSTON HALL

WEDNESDAY, 25th JUNE
AN EVENING WITH
PETE HOBAN
9 p.m. — 11 p.m.

BRIGHTEN UP YOUR MID-WEEK WITH LIVE ENTERTAINMENT AT DALSTON HALL EVERY WEDNESDAY

Tel. Carlisle 710271

Above, Pete (centre) in Carlisle Musical Society's production of Calamity Jane in 1987.

Below, Pete Hoban and the Cliff Eland Big Band line up of 1993.

Pete Hoban singing in the 1970s

James Ivan Hunter

James Ivan Hunter, stage name Van James, had his first music lesson on his thirteenth birthday with Herbert Cartner of River Street, Carlisle. Mr Cartner at that time was the organist for St Aiden's Church.

As Ivan progressed through the Associate Board Grades, Lawrence Foster (brother of Tom, whose dance band regularly played at the Queens Hall) came into his life and introduced him to 'syncopation' and the rhythm, style of playing. He feels a great debt for this to the present day.

At eighteen Ivan was conscripted into the RAF for nearly three years during which time playing was limited to the NAAFI, though his interest took him to the Manchester Palais de Dances where he heard bands such as Levensholme where Bill Gregory fronted an eight brass, five sax, four rhythm line up, and featured visiting bands such as Ted Heath and Tommy Sampson.

On being de-mobbed local piano tuner George Ritchie introduced Ivan to Karl Livock of Newcastle. Karl was a brilliant classical pianist who had studied with Professor York Bowen, and he proceeded to put Ivan on the right path of classical playing. Shortly after Ivan met up with local musicians such as Jimmy Oliver, Peter Hill, George Mitchelhill to name but a

good jobs from it.'

Pete was then approached by Cliff Eland who asked him to fill in for his regular big band singer Alan Buntin who had taken ill. In 1982 Pete came off the road and joined the Cliff Eland Big Band. After Cliff's death in 1995 they were all enthusiastic to keep his memory alive and continue with the band. These days Pete is secretary for the band and provides gigs for the band through his contacts.

Another highlight of Pete's career came in 1999 when he was invited to sing with the BBC Big Band under their conductor Barrie Forgie on a visit to Carlisle.

When big band bookings permit he sings with local band Jazzoo and still has a solo act with mini discs, his forté being Elvis, sounds of the big bands and a bit of country. However the Cliff Eland Big Band takes priority as he admits to still getting a kick out of performing with them and plans to continue to do so.

1952
Melody Maker
NATIONAL
DANCE BAND
CHAMPIONSHIP
•
NORTH BRITAIN
(Eastern)
REGIONAL FINAL
•
Odeon Theatre
Newcastle-on-Tyne
SUNDAY, 21st SEPTEMBER, 1952

few, who were interested in playing modern jazz style. Ivan said, 'We used to rehearse and play in the Milk Bar, Devonshire Street and the Top Hat Club, Blackfriars Street.'

Eventually Ivan was asked by other band leaders to deputise for them when their own pianists were otherwise engaged. Tom Foster, Cliff Eland, Cyril Lowes, George Whitehead (Mayfair and Cameo) and Arthur Douglas being the main names he recalls.

Ivan soon met up with George Baxter (trumpet) and Arthur Ling (tenor) who were keen to form a five-piece band to enter the Melody Maker Contest. So, along with Harold Wilkinson (bass) and Jack Sykes on drums the New Metro Quintet was formed. The band were successful and Ivan was fortunate to win a few 'outstanding musician' awards.

In 1955 Ivan moved to London and was lucky enough to get gigs right away, playing in and around the West End. Unfortunately he contracted tuberculosis in 1958 and was consequently out of work for over two years while he regained his health at a sanatorium at Longtown.

In 1960 he was offered a long summer season with Don Carroll at Carlyon Bay, Cornwall. He accepted this offer along with George Mitchellhill and Bill Thompson, two stalwarts of the Carlisle music scene of that time. After a year in Cornwall, Ivan was

offered a job at the Blackpool Embassy Club by Keith Chalkley and Harvey watson. This lasted several months and was followed by engagements in Liverpool with Mal Craig. This was followed by a period in Yorkshire, playing in Leeds, Bradford, York, Harrogate and Bridlington and most of the 'Yorkshire gold coast' resorts.

When one of the clubs was closed down for financial reasons, Ivan returned to Carlisle. A chance encounter in the street with northern comedian, Bobbie Pattinson, led to more work. Bobbie needed musicians for a nightclub at Crosby on Eden and had also hired Ernie Fox, Jack Sykes on drums and Bernie Cheeseman on bass. At this time when a flood on the River Eden met a high tide, the club was sometimes cut off and patrons had to say overnight.

Shortly after this, another offer came in to play at the 2Bs night club in Scarborough, where Ivan worked for eight years. He then went on tour with comedian Ken Goodwin followed by jobs in summer seasons, pantomimes and nightclubs with stars such as Les Dawson, Norman Wisdom and Bob Monkhouse.

Ivan then went to work for P&O Shipping as musical director on their luxury liners *Canberra* and *Sea Princess*, touring the world for more than three years.

Ivan is now semi-retired and still resides in Scarborough with his family. He considers himself lucky to have always found work doing the job he loves so much and is now in the enviable position of being able to choose the jobs he wants.

The New Metro Quintet with from left, back, Ivan Hunter (piano), Jack Sykes (drums) and Harold Wilkinson (bass) and at the front, George Baxter (trumpet) and Arthur Ling (tenor sax).

Rita Irving

Rita Irving was known to most as a glamourous figure in dancing pumps, putting children through their paces at charity performances given by her Carlisle Dancing School. However people living in the Linstock area during the 1960s may well have seen her clad in overalls and wellington boots, chasing errant cattle up and down the main road, for Rita was equally at home down on the farm.

Mrs Rita Telford, to give her correct married name, was born in Denton Street, Carlisle. Her father was a hatter working for Carricks (later Kangols and today Breed UK) making hats for wealthy clients.

At the age of two Rita began taking dancing lessons at a class run by an Ida Atkins in a bake house in Denton Holme and from then onwards she wanted no other career. Her parents had both been interested in old time dancing and entered many competitions and her grandmother had been a champion clog dancer in Dearham, West Cumberland. Terry, her only brother, was one of the three partners in her dancing school and won a scholarship to study ballet and opera when he came out of the services after the war. He danced with the Royal Ballet and Opera Company within three weeks of joining them.

Rita's school days were spent first at Robert Ferguson School, Denton Holme and then at the County High School. During the school holidays she concentrated on her dancing. She stayed with an aunt in Whitley Bay while she took her certificates in tap, ballet, stage and ballroom dancing, with a local teacher.

At the age of fifteen Rita left school and started work at the Waterton Hall, Warwick Square teaching dancing. A year later she met her husband, Joe

Rita Irving and her daughter Joy, pictured in June 1962.

Telford, at a village dance in Crosby on Eden. Joe was a farmer and with her marriage to him Rita began her own farming career. The couple were married at St Cuthbert's Church, Carlisle, and went to stay with Joe's mother at Oak House, Linstock. They had two children - Joy who became the third partner in the dancing school and Jimmy who later ran the farm.

Sadly Rita is no longer with us but Joy has carried on the family dancing school and still gives dancing classes.

Stewart Jessett

Stewart Jessett began his musical career as a boy vocalist with gang shows in Newcastle in the 1950s. He later played in skiffle groups and took part in a TV series called *Young at Heart* with Jimmy Saville. Stewart joked, 'My late mother said he spoiled my act!'

Later Stewart, who plays the double bass, joined the River Jazz Band and then moved to Carlisle to join another band called the Gelt River Jazz Band, who regularly performed at the Coach House, Headsnook, and the Hayton Lane End during the 1970s. Mick Potts then persuaded Stewart to join his popular Gateway Jazz band and here he stayed until Mick died in April 1993.

With the Gateway band, Stewart played at Royal parties at Windsor Castle as well as having a TV series with Border. The band also made films, records and broadcasts and visited jazz clubs in Holland and at the Edinburgh Festival.

Stewart Jessett

The Gentlemen of Jazz, from left, Jim Harrison, banjo; Dave Taylor, clarinet; Euan Pringle, drums; Stewart Jessett, double bass and Peter Myers, trombone.

Gelt River Jazz Band in 1973, from left, Stewart Jessett, David Taylor and David Carrick.

Stewart, who is also a newsagent in Carlisle, said, 'We always enjoyed ourselves. We played for the love of it and still do. Our late great banjo player, John 'Maitland' Smith, re-formed us into our new and latest band, the Gentlemen of Jazz. We practise every Wednesday night at the Stone Inn, Hayton.' Recently the band appeared with Kenny Ball at Greystoke Castle to raise money for the Carlisle Hospice.

Frank Kenyon

Frank Kenyon was one of Carlisle's best known rock musicians whose career began in the early 60s when he played rhythm guitar for the Ramrods, a band considered to be one of the best in the north.

In October 1963 a rumour went around Carlisle pop circles that Frank was being considered for the Shadows vacancy caused when Bruce Welch decided to quit show business. Frank dismissed it as just that, a rumour.

In 1964 when the Ramrods changed their name and turned fully professional, Frank found himself with the VIPs. They were one of the first Carlisle bands to bask in the international spotlight but sadly they just missed the big time.

After the VIPs split, Frank went on to play with a number of other local bands, most notably Junkyard Angel.

Frank battled against cancer for five months before he died, surrounded by his family, in September 1993, aged 48. Only days earlier he had braved the pain to play for 20 minutes at the Pheasant Inn, Caldewgate, at his own benefit gig, organised by and starring the county's best musicians.

After his death hundreds of friends and fans inundated his wife Norah with cards and flowers. Local musicians organised a 'sell out' tribute concert at the Pirelli Social Club. He was a genuinely nice guy and was much loved on the local music scene.

Frank Kenyon

Bobby Laing

In his early career Bobby Laing worked for the BBC and made several shows such as *What Makes a Star?* He won the Carol Levis discovery show competition and was also winner of three Butlins 'Golden Voice' competitions.

He began singing in 1950 at the Crown and Mitre with the Mayfair Band and quickly became a favourite with the dancers there and at the Cameo Club in Botchergate.

In 1957 he appeared on television with the Joe Loss Band. His ambition was to be a great singer with a successful dance orchestra, but he chose to remain in Carlisle. He lived on Crummick Street and during the day worked as a juke box mechanic.

Bobby Laing, photograph courtesy of the Cumberland Evening News, November 1959.

Below Bobby Laing leads the cast on stage at Her Majesty's Theatre.

Chas Leask

Chas Leask began to take an interest in music in the early 50s when aged just three. While his mother was at work he would spend his days at his Grandma's, where he would listen to dance bands and popular songs on the radio. Through this he discovered rhythm and eventually he taught himself to play the drums. His introductory essay at infant school read, 'My name is Charles Lindsey Leask. I am five years old. My favourite game is Rock 'n Roll.'

At the age of ten or eleven he was influenced by the sounds of Chicago Blues Players, Muddy Waters, Sonny Boy Williamson and John Lee Hooker. Mainstream pop he found questionable, 'I was never really convinced by Cliff Richard but the Shadows were OK.'

In 1962 when the Beatles appeared he recognised the 'weight' in them, similar to the blues men. Other favourite bands were Manfred Mann and most of all the Who. 'I liked the noise of people causing real mayhem through music and I wanted to be one of them. Oh yes! and to attract girls,' he said.

In 1967, whilst a student Chas was looking to join a band when he met Jimmy Atkinson who sang by night and by day pummelled dough in his father's bakery. Chas said, 'People encouraged us so we persuaded guitarists John Potts and David Blackburn to join us. They were both good song writers so we performed their songs, one or two covers and folksongs, although we saw ourselves as an embryonic rock group. To

The Pickwick Paupers, from left, David Blackburn, Jimmy Atkinson, John Potts and Chas Leask.

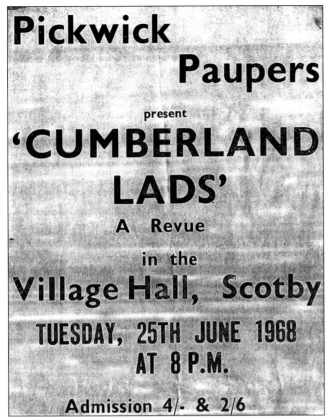

Pickwick
Paupers
present
'CUMBERLAND
LADS'
A Revue
in the
Village Hall, Scotby
TUESDAY, 25TH JUNE 1968
AT 8 P.M.

Admission 4/- & 2/6

and led to a standing ovation at the end of the night.

In August 1968 the band set off for London, reaching their destination in a billow of black smoke from their old van. Chas recalls, 'Whilst in London we appeared at the Mercury Theatre with our show, at London Chalk Farm Roadhouse in John Arden's play, *A Hero Rises up* and we appeared on the TV show *The Market in Honey Lane*, a precursor to *Eastenders* in which we played the part of the Corybrantes, a fictional chart topping, electrically equipped, pop group who were sponsored by one of the Honey Lane regulars when he came into some money. We also appeared on the David Nixon show. He was the most popular magician in the sixties.'

The Pickwick Paupers when they lived in a vicarage in Maida Vale

develop we would play for free at places like the Simon Pringles Square One Folk Club, Carlisle Castle. We needed a name and Pickwick Paupers was settled on despite being an ill-advised pun on Dickens' title and little else. Performance success was measured by a disaster to triumph ratio, leading one fellow performer to announce, 'I'll do my song and then it's Pickwick Lepers."

By 1968 they were doing well and teamed up with programme director Kevin Sheldon at Border Television who was looking for a lead act for his live folk series, *One Evening of Late*. Kevin planned to feature the music, poetry, fans and culture of the growing folk craze and having tasted success with Irish band the Dubliners at Telefis Eirran was keen to repeat the experience. The Paupers were due to appear in all twelve programmes but only did six because of a change of format. The local paper reported, *'One Evening of Late* was pleasantly informal and well packaged. Alas, all that has slipped into the past tense with the show devalued to something closely resembling a campfire soiree with hand clapping, boldly swaying people and combat singing. The Pickwick Paupers, whose sheer enthusiasm and obvious talent had brightened the atmosphere on previous occasions, were gone.'

Kevin stayed with the band and drilled them like a sergeant major for a series of village hall concerts starting at Scotby in June 1968. The shows were a riotous mix of music, sketches and even three acts of *A Midsummer Night's Dream*. Under Kevin's direction the act left the capacity audience crying with laughter

At this time a combination of personality clashes and personal difficulties led John Potts to quit the band. He was replaced by Square One regular John Higgins. 'After several... urgent moves the band found themselves evicted from a tumble down vicarage in Maida Vale by a not very Christian vicar,' joked Chas. So when the opportunity came up to go to work for the Fringe at the Brighton Festival, with accommodation included, they jumped at it, eventually writing and performing a rock musical.

'In Brighton we lived a surreal lifestyle, performing in a huge hall and living in two large houses next door attracting dozens of people for parties. The best thing about the Brighton show was the seating, which was deck chairs. We had the front rows set low and those behind set high. Unbeknown to the audiences money

The Pickwick Paupers at a farewell performance in August 1968 at the Square One Folk Club, Carlisle Castle.

would fall out of their pockets onto the floor, which we duly collected afterwards. This became our income!' said Chas.

At the end of the summer of 1969 it was back to London. Money was still tight so Chas took a job in a restaurant just so he could eat and return home every night with left-overs to feed the band.

Interest had been generated by the rock musical and the band began to gig around England while their agent looked for the right deal. In this time they played Ronnie Scott's Jazz Club, the Marquee Club, Wardour Street, supported Manfred Mann at Southampton University, became a sizeable crowd puller in London jazz and folk clubs, recorded in the Beatles' Abbey Road studio and at the Rolling Stones' Regent Sound studio, which became home less than a decade later to punk. Chas recalls, 'This was a great time, money trickling in, gigs - fun.'

It was then that Chas had the experience of 'meeting the devil at the crossroads'. Chas explains, 'We were given the opportunity to perform our show at the Wimbledon Theatre, prior to a West End opening. The backers wanted to make us household names however the catch was that they only wanted the Pickwick Paupers. The deal did not include my brother Richard, who was our manager or Kevin our director and mentor. That was unacceptable plus I had become bored with the shallow showbiz theatrical side that had been the musical and preferred simply playing gigs and one nighters. So I refused the offer. Not surprisingly the gigs dried up immediately.

'Returning home down the motorway, tired and depressed the band's radio picked up a foreign station at the beginning of a song by the new band King Crimson, *21st Century Schizoid Man,* which seemed to be beamed from another planet. To me it signified the end of my era, my time and the end of the great 60s atmosphere forever. The band did not play again, (us, not King Crimson!)'

However Chas did play again, firstly with an all girl American country rock group, which was signed to the 'hip' Daran Label alongside the likes of Procul Harum. Then he played drums for the Stephen Grapelli Band, making various independent recordings along the way. Next he joined a group called Maxwell Nicholson.

'A book by Hunter Davis became a film and we were given first option to write the music for it. We also released a single through Columbia called *Amaze your Friends.*' recalls Chas.

In 1973 Chas returned to Carlisle. His old band mate Jimmy Atkinson contacted him and they got together as a duo before being joined by John Potts again, then Ian Kellet. This new line up came back as the Paupers. Chas said, 'We virtually invented comedy show groups.

The Pickwick Paupers about to leave for London, 1968.

We rehearsed intensively and became successful all over the north. Our gigs were somewhat wild and dangerous, people would dance on and break tables, damage was done to venues, people were injured and blood was actually spilt. We used to have to return to places to clean up the mess afterwards. I realised I was where I wanted to be - not a theatre star in London, but in a pub in Carlisle wrecking it with my music!'

Members came and went from the Paupers causing the chemistry to be lost and with this Chas lost interest. He played drums for country, jazz and pop bands for a while then in 1980 formed the three piece Doug and the Dragonflies with Ray Begg and Brian Collins both ex-Paupers. Chas said, 'We were fantastically popular and got lots of work.' Illness forced Chas to leave and, on recovering. he played drums and guitar on a deputising basis until at the age of 35 he finally fronted and led as a guitarist with Eddie and the Absconders, the bizarrely named resident band at the Edmund Castle Complex.

After this he went solo, but worsening voice problems forced retirement, although he continued to deputise on drums and guitar. He also began to teach music to various individuals and organisations. Today Chas works at Doug's Guitar Cabin, Houghton, and still teaches music.

Tom Lomas

Tom Lomas is one of the most accomplished and experienced drummers in the area with a career spanning more than 50 years. He first came to Carlisle as an evacuee from Darlington in 1940. He started to play the drums after his favourite uncle taught him as an army cadet in the early 1950s. He learned to read music and to play the tenor horn in the 4th Border Territorial Band.

It was at about this time that Tom teamed up with well known musicians, Dave Batey, and John McKie and Syd Monk, who were both guitarists. After a few months 'jamming', they formed one of Carlisle's first 'skiffle' groups - the Zenith Skiffle Group. About a year later Dave switched to rock 'n roll which was taking the world by storm. From then on they were working non stop, supporting local dance bands and performing in church halls and youth clubs.

Tom then joined the Maurice Petry Trio which played at the Golden Fleece, Ruleholme, in the 1960s and in 1967 he became a founder member of the Border Artistes Theatrical Association.

His first dance band job was as a stand-in drummer for the Edenaires, otherwise known as the Redcoats. This had been his boyhood ambition. He is still playing with the Cliff Eland Band and also pursuing his passion for art by producing fine watercolours.

Tom Lomas

Top, March 1957, playing with the Zenith Skiffle Group

Below, from left Mel Adams (Ian Alcock), Tommy and Doreen Lomas, Maurice and Evelyn Petry, Mark and Mrs Winter at Ruleholme.

Cyril Lowes & the St Stephen's Band.

The St Stephen's Band had its origins in Currock in 1904 when it was connected with St Stephen's Church which stood on James Street and is now a petrol station. In the 1920s the band came under the baton of Mr William Lowes, one of the city's finest musicians. At this time it was renowned as one of the best bands in the whole of Britain. In 1927 and 1929 the band was successful in its attempts to capture the National Championship Shield at Crystal Palace.

The band always had strong family connections, with fathers playing alongside their sons. When William Lowes died in 1956 his son Mr Cyril Lowes took over conductorship of the St Stephen's Band. Cyril was also the conductor of the Carlisle Musical Society and ran the Cyril Lowes Dance Orchestra which was the resident band at the County, Botchergate. Like his father, Cyril was a versatile musician, playing the piano, clarinet, and saxophone as well as brass instruments.

Cyril Lowes was born in the city in 1912. He was educated at St John's School and the Creighton School. Immediately after leaving school he entered into his father's piano tuning business. While at

school Cyril had played in the band as a trombonist and was one of the National Championship winning team.

In the late 1950s and early 1960s concern was expressed at a lack of interest in brass bands, but Carlisle's St Stephen's Band helped to put over to the public the new look brass band. The band together with the Carlisle Musical Society would perform 'songs from the shows'. At first members of the

Pictured above, Cyril Lowes

Below, the winning team proudly showing off the shield won at the National Championships, Crystal Palace, London. The band is pictured outside Carlisle Market where they rehearsed. Cyril Lowes is the middle trombonist in the second row.

TONIGHT.. COME DANCING
to
Cyril Lowes' Dance Orchestra
in the
County Ballroom
FREE BUFFET ———— BAR
To everyone who enjoys true Ballroom Dancing, why not make Tuesday Night at the County your weekly rendezvous
8 p.m. to Midnight   Admission 5/-

Mr S. Little   Mr R. West   Mr W. James   Mr H. Routledge

Musical Society were apprehensive fearing the sound of the band would drown out their voices, however it proved to be a popular and marvellous combination.

In October 1965 the St Stephen's Band travelled to London to play in the National Championships, hoping to return with the treasured silver trophy. There were 25 musicians making the journey under band master Mr Cyril Lowes and five of them had 237 years service between them - Billy James, solo cornet with 46, Stanley Little, baritone trombone with 46, Harold Routledge, soprano trombone with 44, Cyril himself with 45 and his uncle Bert with 56 years.

Mr Cyril George Lowes died in March 1970 at the age of 58 years leaving his widow and one son, Geoffrey, who played trombone with the St Stephen's Band. After Cyril's death the band came under the baton of Ifor James the world famous French horn player.

Pictured clockwise, from top:

Four members of the championship St. Stephen's Band

December 1971 and Ifor James conducts the band ready for a concert in Preston.

The 1972 trombone section of St Stephen's Band, from left, Geoffrey Lowes (Cyril's son), Norman Hodgson and Cliff Attwood, who now leads the Cliff Eland Band. Photograph courtesy of Cumbrian Newspapers.

Members of the band look over the music with Cyril Lowes (centre)

Cyril Lowes conducting the St Stephen's Silver Band at the Currock House Community Centre Carnival in June 1959.

Peter McCaffery

Peter McCaffery, was born in 1951,making him one of the 'youngsters' of this book and takes us into the 1970s.

Peter acquired his first guitar at the age of fifteen. He was largely self taught although he did visit music teacher Billy Stewart of Dias' shop a couple of times. However being influenced by the likes of Cliff and the Shadows, the Beatles and local innovators such as Jim Henshaw of the VIPs and Malcolm Mason of Lemongrass he found Billy a bit old fashioned so never went back.

Peter enjoyed watching the television show *Thank Your Lucky Stars* and, closer to home, Peter was influenced by his cousin, Tommy Kennedy of the BATS. Peter recalls, 'Tom and a few friends would arrive at my parents' house for a get together and a good sing-a-long and before long the neighbours and passers by would join in.'

It was through Tommy that Peter became involved in BATs charity concerts. The family still have keepsakes of Tommy's days on stage in the shape of a hat and microphone.

In 1970 Peter got together with Roger Crosby, Billy Curry and Billy Nobel to form the band Preview. He said, 'We didn't set out to get a recording contract or

Preview, back, Roger Crosby and Billy Curry with Peter McCaffery and Billy Nobel.

to become famous, we just did it all for the enjoyment. Besides once you were in a group locally you were thought of as a celebrity. We would practise at least once a week in the local youth clubs. You could see a different group there just about every night. Initially we were all pals together on a great adventure it was the usual money factor which caused personnel clashes which led to personnel changes and a new name Goldy.

Peter aged fifteen in 1966 at the back door of ex-Carlisle Mayor Hughie Little's house. The photograph was taken by Donald Little.

130

Goldy, Billy Curry, Peter McCaffery, Tony Hill and Mick Shannon.

Peter recalls, 'Initially the starting point for everyone was the village hall dances, such as the Victory Hall, Dalston, which we got through Monica Linton of CES Entertainments. The village hall dances usually didn't start until quite late. It was soft drinks only, with tea and sandwiches provided in the interval. As no alcohol was served at these functions, the locals would roll in from nearby pubs all ready for a 'good hop and a fight'. Fights usually broke out because local lads would get jealous of their lasses fancying the lads in the group. It wasn't all rock 'n roll, we also had to include music for the older ones to waltz to.

'The next move was into the working mens and social clubs, booked through Andy Park. We worked the circuit known as the 'gold coast'. This included the likes of Silloth, Maryport, Workington and Whitehaven, which at that time were all thriving communities, due to full employment in the steel and mining industries.

'We never got paid a great amount. In those days fees for a supporting group were £18 and £22 for a top group, less 10% commission, of course. Looking back we were all financially naive and were probably getting ripped off. Hence, we never had enough money to buy top equipment so we went along to Jimmy Dias' shop and bought it all on hp, the same as everyone else was doing at the time. Equipment in the early 70s ranged from an average 40 watt PA system to the top 100 watt, powered by valves. The equipment used these days are PAs of at least 1000 watts, powered by transistors.

'None of us had telephones so we would meet in local pubs to discuss ways and means to get our next bookings. One of our biggest problems was transport, none of us had any or could drive. In those days you could say we got to our bookings 'on a wing and a prayer'. It involved a lot of hard work but was a lot of fun along the way, all I ever wanted to do was to play good music.'

Stan McManus

Stan McManus as a professional footballer.

Stan McManus, known to everyone as 'Stan the Man' was also well known for his catch phrase, 'Would I tell a lie?' is still enjoying a career which has spanned over 60 years.

Born in October 1932, Stan began entertaining at an early age. He recalls, 'In those days entertainment began at home with all your relatives gathered around the old piano. My speciality was to perform a tap dance in my clogs and to sing *Jeepers Creepers where did you get those Peepers*.'

Having being inspired by Fred Astaire's performance in the film *Top Hat* which he had seen at the Public Hall, Stan began to teach himself to tap dance. His first public appearance was at the age of eleven when he appeared as Mrs Aladdin in a youth club pantomime. He then teamed up with Michael McKie with whom he would busk for the queues outside the city's cinemas for pennies.

In the late 1940s Stan went into the forces. After

Cliff Eckersley and Stan McManus in the bar of their Upstairs Club, Lowther Street.

Two of the characters Stan played while working at the Lido, Silloth.

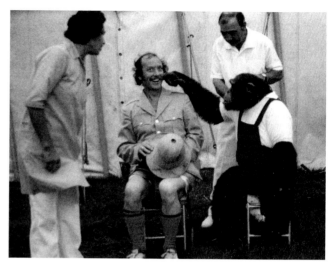

Stan appearing at Carlisle's first Great Fair with the PG Tips' chimpanzee.

completing his training at Blandford, he was then stationed at Ashford, Kent, finally ending up at Catterick in North Yorkshire, where he became camp entertainer alongside Jack Warner of *The Blue Lamp* film, who later played in *Dixon of Dock Green*.

During his time in the forces Stan developed his interest in football, eventually turning professional on being de-mobbed. As a professional footballer he played for Bury, Southport, Queen of the South and Carlisle United in the days when Bill Shankley was manager.

On his return to Carlisle he became a salesman by day and an entertainer by night, becoming 'King Bat' with the Border Artistes and Theatrical Society, which saw him along with other BATs members perform at many charitable functions.

At one time Stan ran the Pheasant Pub, Caldewgate, and co-owned with Cliff Eckersley, the local night club known as the Upstairs Club, Lowther Street. 'We were the first club to bring top names like Frank Carson and Norman Collier into the city,' said Stan.

For 25 years Stan was compere, comedian and entertainments manager at the Solway Lido, Silloth, where many a good night out was to be had for both locals and holidaymakers. Over the years Stan recalls compering for numerous big names such as Andy Cameron, Donald Peers, Vince Hill, Ken Dodd, Matt Munro, Frankie Vaughan, Dickie Valentine, to name but a few.

'I appeared 20 years ago with the Mersey Beat at Wigton Gala and I am reappearing this June (2003) with them at Silloth Rotary Club,' said Stan, 'One very memorable moment was when I appeared on the stage at Carlisle's first Great Fair with the original PG Tips chimpanzee. As you can see from the photograph, I have my hat tightly held over my privates. That's because the chimp kept trying to grab them, and I can tell you he had a vice like grip!'

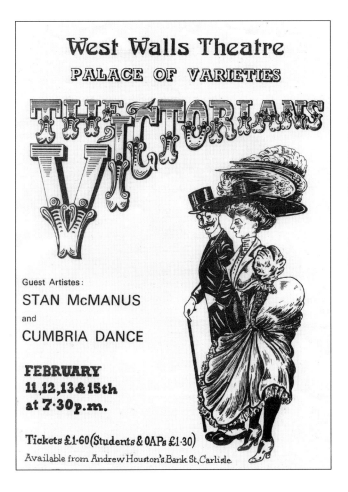

In the 1980s Stan became part of Gil Johnstons the Gill Billies. 'We were a fun group, touring the country pubs. I can tell you many an act followed us on stage and wished they hadn't.'

Stan 'the Man' McManus is still enjoying his career as are his audiences. During his career he has tap danced on every stage and table top in Carlisle, and has performed a large percentage of his work for charity functions. He has helped raise between £60,000 and £70,000 for good causes, such as Guide Dogs for the Blind, and not least of these being his involvement for 31 years (never missing a year) in the pensioners' Christmas shows, where he regularly has them 'rolling in the aisles' with his antics.

Below, celebrating 25 years as an entertainer at the pensioners' Christmas party.

Ena Mitchell

Ena Mitchell was born and lived most of her life in Carlisle, singing from an early age. Her first singing teacher was Ann Fiddler, followed by training in Edinburgh for six years. On her return to Carlisle, she started singing with the Carliol Choir. She continued with this choir and became president before she retired in July 1961. On her retirement, she said, 'I have been a very lucky woman. My profession has given me every honour, so I have decided to retire when I am still at my best.'

After retiring from the choir she went to teach in Glasgow and Manchester.

She married William James who was a member of St Stephen's Band for many years and their son, Ivor, became a horn player with the Hallé Orchestra. Tragically the couple died with two days of each other in the late 1970s.

Ivor James, son of the famous singer, Ena Mitchell, photographed in May 1954 with the Hallé Orchestra.

George Mitchelhill

George Mitchelhill was born in 1932, is affectionately known locally as 'Mad Mitch' and is a prominent local musician with a larger than life character.

George took up a hobby that was to turn into a career, when he learned to play the drums with the Boys Brigade at the age of eleven and, while a pupil at the Creighton School, he played with the city's Boys Brigade Band.

His big break came when he began playing with the Cliff Eland Dance Band. In the mid-1950s he became a founder member, with Mick and Al Potts, of Carlisle's Jazz Club.

'Mad Mitch' in April 1996.

At the age of 30, in May 1962, he left his job at John Laing's and became a full time professional. The following year he travelled to Cornwall, which at the time was hailed as 'the millionaires' playground'. He opened at the huge Cornish Riviera Club at Carlyon Bay, a beauty spot near St Austell, with his own highly successful quartet playing for dining, dancing and cabaret. An enthusiastic George recalls, 'I loved it down there. It was hard work, seven nights a week, the place seldom slackened, but it was very rewarding.'

Carlisle pianists Ivan Hunter and Arthur Curwen have also played at the same club, and local tenor sax player, Dave Batey played as a guest artist there with George's quartet. Shortly before returning with his family to Carlisle in October 1963 George was presented

George Mitchelhill on the drums with Ivan Hunter on piano.

with a tie bearing the county insignia of Cornwall and made an honourary citizen of the county in recognition of his charity work in the south west.

When he returned to Carlisle in between seasons he would spend part of the day at the Dias' Music Shop demonstrating drum kits. Many people will recall George from the days when he worked at the men's outfitters shop of Tom Purves & Sons, the 'Artistic Tailors' which was situated next to the 101/Talk of the Border club on Botchergate. Geoff recalls, 'We used to go there to get our shirts with cut away collars to accommodate our Windsor knotted ties, which were all the rage at the time.' Many a time George would give impromptu drum lessons or have customers in fits of laughter with his jokes.

Locally he has played for various outfits over the years. His duo with Dave Batey became very popular featuring George drumming and wise cracking to the amusement of their audiences. The Mel and Mitch duo was equally popular, (Mel being Mel Adams whose real name was Ian Alcock). George remembers that the highlight of his career was working for the late, great Ray Ellington, of the *Goon Show* fame, and the hardest person to work for was Freddie Starr. Although he is now in his retirement George still enjoys an occasional drum session.

The Nomads

The Nomads were formed in 1960 in St Ann's Hill, Carlisle, by two close friends, Alec Alves and Ernie Green. Teaching themselves guitar, they learned various songs by artists such as Cliff Richard, the Everly Brothers, Chuck Berry and the Shadows. Adding a drummer, John Porthouse, another St Ann's lad, and a bass player, Alan McCubbin, from Wigton Road, the Nomads, were formed. Rehearsals took place in Alec's kitchen and dining room.

By 1961 they went from acoustic to electric guitars, and now had the use of St Augustine's church hall, Briar Bank, for rehearsals, sharing it with another Carlisle group, the Teen Combo. In 1961 the Nomads made their first public appearance at the Etterby Mission Hall Youth Club, playing a selection of songs and instrumental pop chart tunes. Being successfully received by the audience they rehearsed intensively and were becoming proficient and confident.

The Nomads at the time when they changed their name to the Relics, from left, Ernie Green, Stewart Kenyon, Ian Grant, Gerry Ward and Alec Alves.

In 1961/62 the first personnel change came to the Nomads when Alan McCubbin, the bass player left and Les Dock, from Currock, an old school friend of Alec took up the bass player's position.

The next big step was the Nomads' first professional appearance which took place at the Cameo Ballroom, Botchergate. The Cameo at this time was an upstairs dance hall and featured the Cliff Eland Band as resident dance band, playing foxtrots, waltzes, quicksteps, jives and dance band classics of the day. As the Nomads were plugging in their electric equipment, Alec still remembers a conversation with Cliff Eland on the lines, 'Cliff- 'This electric music will never take off!'. Alec - 'Wait and see!' The Nomads played for an hour, and the reception was incredible. We were asked to return at the grand fee of twelve

The Relics in 1964, clockwise from back, Ernie Green, Alec Alves, Ian Grant and Terry Ward.

shillings and six pence (62p). Success at the Cameo established the Nomads as a known group.'

In 1962 Alec and Ernie went to see a local dance hall promoter, Rita Irving, who held teenage dances in the City Hall in Castle Street and the Queen's Hall in West Walls. The Nomads auditioned for Rita which resulted in regular bookings from her at the Queen's Hall and the Gretna Hall, over the next two years, along with other groups such as the Ramrods, the Danubes, Four Dollars, Fire and the Ferinos, Me and the Moonlighters and the Corals. Groups by this time had become the hub of entertainment in Carlisle, and there were at least twenty different outfits.

Alec and Ernie were ambitious to match the Ramrods, who were the best local group, and there were personnel changes within the Nomads. John Porthouse was replaced by Mostyn Carpenter, another St Ann's Hill resident, who had been tutored and coached by Carlisle legend George Mitchellhill and Les Dock was replaced by Ian Grant, from Harraby.

By 1964 the group progressed and played at many dance halls and clubs. Jerry Ward, again from Harraby was added to the line up as second guitarist, to free Ernie Green to be front singer. Amongst the venues played were the Queen's Hall, the Gretna Hall, the County Hall, Harraby Catholic Club (a wooden shed), along with the Railway Club and Upperby Institute.

At this time the group spread its wings and travelled to venues in Millom, Barrow, Stranraer, Brampton,

Kendal, Egremont and in Scotland. Alec's two fondest memories are Egremont, where they were the support band to Johnny Kidd and the Pirates (a big name) and Newcastle University where they supported the Four Pennies who had just reached No 1 in the charts with *Juliet*. The Nomads had by now changed their name to the Relics. Mostyn Carpenter left the group in 1964, disappearing down a side street in London never to be seen again. He was replaced by Stuart Kenyon, who drummed for the group's remaining life.

By mid-1964 the Relics were in crisis. Personality clashes were appearing between Alec and Ernie, and the group itself was having problems with equipment and instruments. In October 1964 everything came to a head in Annan, when all the amplification equipment failed, and the Relics had to run the gauntlet of angry fans and escape the building. Annan was the last (none) appearance of the Nomads/Relics.

After the demise of the group, Alec went to college to study to be a librarian, Ernie Green and Ian Grant became, with others the Brothers Grimm, Jerry ward retired for a while and Stuart Kenyon joined other local groups.

BEAT! BEAT! BEAT!

RODNEY WARR INVITES ALL MODS, ROCKERS and MIDS TO "POP-INN" TO THE

COUNTY BALLROOM

THIS WEEK-END

FRIDAY NIGHT, MAY 8th—

Proudly announcing a new name for one of Carlisle's foremost groups. From henceforth

THE RELICS

(formerly the Nomads)

plus

PAUL CRAVEN and THE GRAVEDIGGERS

"Man, you'll dig this lot!"

7.30 p.m. to Midnight. 4½ Hours' Shaking. Only 3/- Admission.

SATURDAY, MAY 9th—

Presenting a return visit at your request of popular

BENNY SKY and the FENTONS

plus

"CITY SOUNDS," featuring 'DOLLY, THE MOD.'

7.30 p.m. to 11.30 p.m. 4 Hours' Shake Down. Only 4/- Admission.

Maurice Petry

Maurice Petry was born on 21 December 1942 in Longtown. He recalls, 'Ever since I was a wee boy I would hear my mother always singing so I have always sung too. At school I would sing in school plays. I also sang with the Longtown Choir. I was brought up with Dave Storey, we were the Longtown lads.'

Maurice taught himself to play the guitar. His early career began in 1958/1959 at Eden Youth Club Centre, which was situated at the NAAFI Club, where he would play the guitar and sing solo or with Dave Storey.

Early in 1960 he was singing at the Bush, Longtown, when he was approached by a Mr Hay of Kirklinton Hall. He asked him if he would like to make himself £5 so he went along to play. At Kirklinton he met

Tommy Kennedy, whom he would meet up with again and work with many times in the future. Maurice has also worked with many other local entertainers.

In July 1964, encouraged by his grandfather, Maurice entered and won the *High Hopes* competition and went on to become the outright winner of *Cock o' the Border* two of Border Television's first talent shows. By now he was working in clubs both local and as far afield as Manchester.

Maurice is probably best remembered locally for his time at the Golden Fleece, Ruleholme, where he was resident singer six nights a week during the 1960s. It was there that he was credited as setting the standard of entertainment in the area and met Harold Muir, who worked with the first resident band, known as the Ruleholme Band. When Harold left, the band was joined by Tommy Lomas.

After the Ruleholme days Maurice remained working on the scene, for a long time on his own. In 1967, Maurice, together with

Below, the Maurice Petry Trio at Ruleholme.

137

Maurice when he won the 'High Hopes' competition.

Ritchie Jefferson, Tom Lomas and a number of other well known local artistes, such as Bobby Laing, Rodney Warr, Jean Johnstone and Tommy Kennedy, formed the Border Artistes Theatrical Society, (BATS), although all working professionally would stage concerts in aid of charities.

Maurice was one of the outstanding talents of the 1960s and he is still going strong. He has recently teamed up with Gordon Norman, and the pair go by the name of Petrified.

Mick Potts

Mick Potts was a born musician and when just a small boy would play notes on the spout of a watering can, graduating later to a bird cage stand. Improvisation having overtaken him so early, the freedom of expression jazz music afforded was an automatic outlet.

He started playing the piano at the age of seven and won many prizes at musical festivals. At this time he was introduced to Benny Goodman, Harry James, Count Basie and a host of others via 78 rpm records. By the age of eleven he was playing Boogie Woogie piano on Sunday afternoons at the City Picture House Cafe.

When Mick was fourteen, while still a pupil of Carlisle Grammar School, he was playing trumpet in a band which played for personal pleasure at any available venue, including private houses, lecture halls and reading rooms. Playing trumpet however was a necessity rather than a personal choice, as there was nobody else available he buckled to and taught himself. From this stage Mick and jazz became synonymous in the Carlisle area and many other places.

In the autumn of 1954 Mick Potts co-founded along with Arthur 'Danny' Curwen the Garret Jazz Club in Devonshire Street. Mick and the Gateway Jazz Band played with and opposite many of the jazz greats including Sidney Betchet, Louis Armstrong, George Chisholm, George Melly and many more. In January 1958 he appeared with his Gateway Jazz Band on a BBC television programme the *Six Five Special*.

Mick Potts in action.

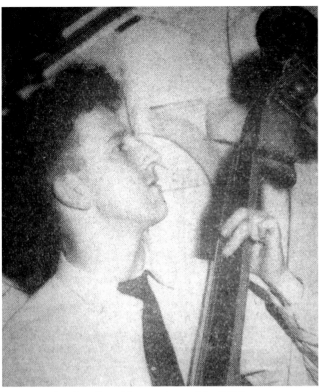

Eric Smith who played bass, pictured in 1958.

Top right, the Gateway Jazz Band playing in a disused quarry near Warnell Fell in August 1965.

Below, from left, Norman Heeley-Creed, Jim Willis, John Smith, Miick Potts, Al Potts and Peter Myers

Locally Mick and his band would play up in the fells for jazz enthusiasts, on steamboats in the Lake District and even hiring a whole train for railroad jazz raves.

In 1978 Mick was the star of the Border Television programme *Take the Mick*. The programme was shown all over the country and even overseas. Although Mick never got to New Orleans he did appear on television there. Following the programme's success Mick and the Gateway Jazz Band were invited by Prince Philip to play at Windsor Castle, perhaps the crowning glory of their career. The Duke describing them as, 'his favourite jazz band'.

The band also developed a fruitful relationship with the great George Chisholm, resulting in an album recorded live at the Rosehill Theatre in 1978.

Above, Mick Potts and the Gateway Jazz Band when they appeared at Windsor Castle at the request of the Duke of Edinburgh.

Below, George Chisholm and Mick Potts

Below right, Cockermouth Railway Station 'Railway Rave'

Mick, who died in 1993, never tired of playing and he toured schools and colleges spreading the fun of jazz. He was never interested in the politics of music; he was in it to entertain and to enjoy. Certainly Mick and his band were not interested in financial gain, in fact any fee usually went back over the bar.

He played on both trumpet and piano with different bands in different styles. He was best described by Portcullis in the *Carlisle Journal* of March 1965 as, 'Ebullient, effervescent, energetic, occasionally egotistical, sometimes exasperating, always entertaining, the epitome of jazz music in the area. Such is Mick Potts leader of the Gateway Jazz Band.'

Apart from his life in jazz, Mick had many other interests. He was the chairman and managing director of Robert Todd and Sons, the woollen spinners in Shaddongate, home of Dixon's chimney. A legendary salesman, he was well known and respected throughout the international textile world. He often combined his jazz and his business. At one time he owned two nightclubs in Carlisle, one of which was the infamous Micks One, opened by Mick so the Gateway would have a regular Sunday night venue.

Mick's diverse taste in music led him to present a regular radio show called *First Time Around* in which he reviewed new jazz releases.

Raymond Purves

Raymond Purves was born in Edinburgh. His family came to Carlisle when he was fifteen and Raymond finished off his schooling at Ashley Street School. His grandmother, also from Edinburgh, was a music teacher who taught him to play the piano.

Raymond also played the accordion and performed with the Pat Allen Dance Team and Derek Batey, who was a ventriloquist. He would sometimes play with Derek Batey at the Swiss Court. He also played drums for the Railroaders and for the United Servicemen's Club resident trio with Lance Armstrong and Gordon Halliwell. He even played in the local TA Band.

Raymond played all over Cumbria with the Skyliners and Railroaders and once had a two week stint playing the drums in Benidorm filling in for the usual drummer, who was ill. He declined to take on the job full time.

He had a variety of day jobs, including working for the railway, driving instruction, driving a bread van and, for fifteen years, he was a financial consultant for Pearl Insurance.

The Cameo was always a special place for him, for it was there that he met Moira, marrying her twelve weeks later. When he died of cancer at the age of 57 in May 1995 Moira received hundreds of cards from the many people he had come to know over the years.

Raymond's daughter, Mrs Heather Cowperthwaite said, 'He really loved all kinds of music - even the sort I bought and brought home when I was a girl. It seemed as if everyone in Carlisle knew my dad and it's always nice to hear them say what a nice lad he was and a good drummer too.'

Moira said, 'Ray left a grand daughter, Jade who is also a music fan and his grandson Dean plays guitar. He always lived life to the full - he especially loved his music and holidays abroad. He knew he wasn't well, but went along to see Heather and his son-in-law, Steve, who had a piano in the front room. For a full half hour he played non-stop, after that he never played again. He always had a smile and a kind word for everyone. He was our Mr Music.'

Above, Ray pictured when he was in the TA. Heather said, 'He was stationed over in Germany but he was recalled back to Carlisle as they had no one else to play the bugle.'

Ray Purves, left, playing with the Skyliners in the old Silver Grill on English Street.

The Ramrods

The Ramrods were an excellent line up consisting of Jim Henshaw on lead guitar and leader of the group, Frank Kenyon on rhythm guitar, Walter Johnson on drums and singer Mike Harrison. They started on the beat scene in 1960 with Alf Ridley, bass guitarist, joining in September 1963. It was success from the beginning with the group going to the top of the popularity poll in the Border region. They won talent contests up and down the country.

In August 1963 the Ramrods put their own time and cash into an attempt to reach the big time. They hired a room in West Walls to build a recording studio complete with echo chamber and sound making equipment. The walls were covered in egg cartons to deaden the noise.

Jimmy Henshaw said, ' We felt we got the correct

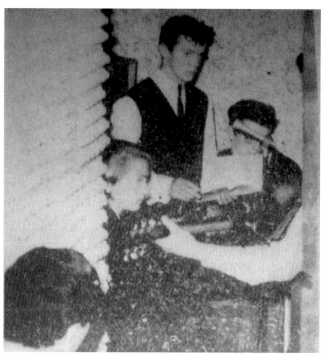

sound. It's the way some of the big groups had rocketed to success.' They played at two or three dances a week and pooled their money, several times a week, working to complete the studio. On the studio's completion they taped several of their numbers and sent them off to recording companies.

Alec Alves of the Nomads and the Relics said that they shared the rehearsal rooms with the Ramrods. 'The top room at West Walls was previously the Carlisle Spiritualist Church. I remember some strange happenings. For instance, our equipment would be moved around and we knew no one else had been up there,' said Alec.

In 1964 the Ramrods changed their name to the VIPs and turned fully professional.

The Ramrods in 1963, from left, Dave McComiskey, Walter Johnson, Frank Kenyon and Jim Henshaw. Dave left Carlisle for Liverpool and went on to join Casey Jones and the Engineers, playing alongside Eric Clapton and Tom McGuiness. He later moved to America where he still lives today. Photograph courtesy of Norah Kenyon.

Top, The Ramrods building their own studio.

142

Tony Renney

Tony Renney, wrote that the real heroes of the era were people like Jim Henshaw and the VIPs. 'When I was just a lad learning the trade, they were true pros, touring Europe and making records in the days when it was a real honour to do so, and you had to go to London to do it. Nowadays, when every pub singer makes a CD, people forget what an achievement it was back then, and lads like Jim did it. They were the leaders and the likes of me only followed in their footsteps in later years.'

Tony was introduced to the piano at an early age by his father, Mr Anthony Renney and became a pupil of George Atkinson of Maryport. Tony's first love is country music.

He continues, 'I started in 1962, just schoolboy groups at first. I do remember playing on Rodney Warr Promotions in Carlisle as a member of TNT on Saturday 6 November 1966, the all day 'Golden Gate' pop group contest in Carlisle Market Hall. Other groups included Electrons, Invaders, Westerners, DJs, Arizonas, Pieces of Eight, the Dolls and Wee Willie Hendry's Wanderers. The Invaders won senior section and TNT won the junior section. Donald Peers presented us with the prize. Also with TNT I remember playing at weekly beat dances in Cummersdale

Tony Renney

Embassy Ballroom around the same time.

'On 20th August 1966 there was a pop group contest in Hall Park, Workington with all the local groups. The Invaders won, with TNT second. Later in 1966 TNT disbanded when we all left school and went away to our various colleges and universities. As luck would have it I went to Liverpool, joined a group there and was able to partake in the last fading years of the Mersey sound playing such places as the original Cavern, though by then of course big names like the Beatles were long gone and times were changing in music.

Tony Renney is still performing today as part of the Carlisle based duo South of the Border.

In 1983 Tony Renney achieved the cap and gown diploma and letters of association to the London College of Music examinations on the classical guitar. At the time Tony already held two special certificates from the Royal School of Music for passing all the highest grades of the school examinations in guitar playing and the theory of music.

I returned to Workington in 1968, took up country music and joined the Lofthouse Cowboys who were resident in the Lofthouse Motel, Bothel. Personnel over the years included Chris Graham, Derek Tolson, Dennis Blamire, Stan Watson, Tex McEating and Arnold Miller. As well as the house band, the Lofthouse was a meeting place for local country musicians, and jam sessions were frequent, with Mel Adams being one particularly talented musician who joined in. It was long before line dancing was ever heard of. I remember tremendous nights in the fantasy wild west atmosphere of the Lofthouse, with wonderful food being served by Jean Rigg and the whole building shaking to a packed crowd wildly dancing to the Lofthouse Cowboys frantically blasting out western songs like *Ghost Riders in the Sky*.

'In 1970 Chris, Dennis, Derek and myself left the Lofthouse (which later burned down) and together with drummer Colin Wright renamed ourselves the Saddlers. Over the next few years we were extremely busy all over the north of England and Scotland as a modern country music band.

'In 1975 I left the Saddlers to turn professional with a London band Bryan Chalker's New Frontier, recording, broadcasting and touring all over Britain and Europe. I returned to Cumbria in 1980 and joined the Scottish recording group Country Breeze who at the time had a recording contract and a hit album in the British Country music charts.

Rue and the Rockets

Rue & the Rockets are a classic rock 'n roll band who, having been on the road for 40 years are possibly Britain's longest surviving rock band. Rueben (drums), Jimmy (guitar) and Alan (guitar), the Slater brothers, are also the proud owners of a travelling fair inherited as a family concern. 'One minute we're in sequinned costumes, and the next we're in overalls dismantling dodgem cars,' said Rue, 'As youngsters we dismantled and made trumpets out of organ pipes. That old organ would probably be worth a fortune today.'

Their father was an amateur fiddler and he always wanted his sons to have music lessons. So they went to Billy Stewart's Music Academy, above Dias' Music Shop, Carlisle. Rueben started on guitar and accordion, then switched to the drums, encouraged by George Mitchellhill and Jimmy took up the guitar.

What's in a name? Well, Rue is obviously taken from Rueben, and the Rockets part, well that comes from the name of the steam traction engine which was used on the Slaters' fair. Jimmy said, 'My father actually paid to have two traction engines, including the Rocket taken away when we had no further use for them. We've just heard that the Rocket has recently been sold for £185,000.'

Rue and the Rockets had their beginnings back in the sixties when Rueben Slater was only twelve years old. He had played for his own amusement but then they decided to go public and, after lot of hard work and disappointment, they rose to become Carlisle's top pop outfit of 1963. Jimmy Slater, lead, Alan Slater, bass, Rueben Slater drums, Gerald Batey, piano and clavioline and Henry Codona, vocalist, were all brought up in show tradition, touring the fairground circuit.

Gerald Batey was brought in to take the place of Brian Codona who was part of the group but left to get married and went to live in Newcastle in 1963.

At only 4ft 8" Rueben or 'Tiny Rue' as he was called had a reputation as one of the brightest drummers around at the time. The Rockets were managed by Rodney Warr, who did a tour of the Border towns with them to get them established. After an appearance on Border TV with Eden Kane, the Rockets never looked back. In September 1964 they were voted 'Top of the Pops' for 'unknown' groups in the beat magazine *Mirabelle*.

The Slater boys would get hundreds of letters from their girl fans requesting jobs working on the fair to be near the Rockets. They were mobbed so many times

Rue and the Rockets in the early 60s, from left, Gerald Batey, Jimmy, Alan and Reuban Slater.

that 'Little Rue' decided to get all the body building exercise he could, saying, 'Believe me it's tough at the top.'

In March 1964 they signed two important contracts, one of them being to appear with Brian Poole and the Tremeloes. Rueben hit the front page of the Sunday Sun in 1964 when shrieking fans stopped the traffic in Newcastle City Centre. After a matinee performance at the Majestic Ballroom in Westgate he had to be guarded back stage for almost an hour. Rue recalls, 'It was a scary experience. The girls ripped the sleeves off my gold lamé jacket and my clothes were being torn to pieces. I had to leave the place on top of our van so they couldn't reach me. We were barred from appearing on Saturdays in Newcastle after that due to hysterical fans blocking the streets.'

In winter they would do gigs all over the north of England and southern Scotland sometimes five or six

Above, Rue and the Rockets, July 1966

Left, Reuban Slater, February 1966

Right, Rodney Warr with Rue and the Rockets, June 1969

Below, Rue and the Rockets, Jimmy, Alan and Reuban.

Mobbed after a concert in Newcastle, the band had to make their getaway on the van roof

times a week. In the summer the fair would take over from the singing. They have done gigs at all the clubs, working men's clubs, leek shows, pigeon suppers, cabaret, wherever people wanted them. 'In fact there's no place in Carlisle we've not played, even at Upperby Men's Institute when it was just a shed,' said Rueben.

After signing up with Top Rank they went on to play all the major venues across the north including Newcastle's Mayfair, the Go Go Club, which was owned by the Animals' manager and the Stockton Globe. They were also signed up with the prestigious Fontana Record Label to record their debut single *Sleepwalk* at Marble Arch Studios, London.

Rue recalls, 'Locally Duncan McKinnon from Melrose was the man. He brought in a lot of big names and acts to Carlisle. We have played with some of the most successful bands of the 60s including the Animals, the Searchers, the Hollies; we toured with the Rolling Stones and the Kinks. In fact we have played with everyone except the Beatles.' However the fab four did stay in a Musicians' Union guesthouse in Newcastle's West End at the same time as Rue and the Rockets. Once Rue saved the day for Irish rocker Van Morrison when the Rockets supported his band. They also stood in for Manfred Mann over in the North East for a 3000 strong crowd and got paid just £35.

The band has stuck together and built a huge fan base across the north and beyond for one of their latest hits, *Sticky Vicky in Benidorm*. This has become the number one Benidorm record. Rue said, 'We have worked really hard and we still do. We do music from the 60s, 70s and 80s, but mostly we do our own stuff. Even now we pack out venues because fans we had from the 60s still come to see us. We finish with real rock 'n roll and even the younger ones love it.'

Donald Scott

Donald Scott was born 23rd April 1937. His career had its beginnings in the 1940s when he was encouraged by his grandma to play the upright piano in her Watson Street home. He began taking piano lessons when aged about ten with Peter Evans, musical director for Her Majesty's Theatre, followed by lessons from Frank Radcliffe, the last full time organist at the Lonsdale Cinema.

Donald played the harmonium in his Redbank School chapel and the organ at Rydal Street Methodist Church. He also enjoyed appearing in his school pantomimes.

At the age of sixteen he began his first show business partnership, with

Elizabeth Stewart. They won a £7.50 second prize in a 1953 talent contest. Throughout the 1950s they played in hundreds of working men's clubs in Cumberland and Westmorland. They would do cabaret evenings in venues such as the Silver Grill Restaurant. They also performed for the BBC Northern Home Service. In 1958 they performed in the 'Pick of the Towns' show in Her Majesty's Theatre, encouraged by the manager John Sullivan. Donald recalls, 'The late fifties were exciting times, we were lucky in having such a grand theatre.'

Donald and Liz also appeared on Border TV's *Focus* programme during the station's first week of broadcasting in September 1960.

Donald then joined Carlisle Light Operatic Society and played character parts in *Bless the Bride*, *The*

Above, Donald as Gladys May

Below, Donald at the organ in Rydal Street Methodist Chapel

Elizabeth Stewart and Donald Scott

Maid of the Mountain and The Merry Widow. He then went on to join the Gilbert and Sullivan Choral Society who performed in the City Hall, where he played all the comedy roles.

He played piano for the Ronnie Hodgson Accordion Band prior to joining the Alf Adamson Orchestra. Donald recalls he was doing the cabaret with Liz Stewart one night in the Crown & Mitre, on their return from the interval break Alf Adamson asked Donald if he would stand in for George Fehrenbach the pianist, who was late back from the break. Donald was only too pleased to do so. About a week later he was painting a mural in a house on Howe Street when Alf pulled up outside in his car and told Donald that George had had a heart attack and asked if he would like to join the orchestra. He agreed, considering it a great honour, and stayed with Alf until the band was wound up in 1972.

Donald hosted the radio programme Songs for Sunday from 1977-1983 and in the 1980s the Donald Scott in Concert series became a success. This introduced the common-as-muck Scott family including his popular Gladys May character. His inspirations for comedy came from everyday life observations. The series was axed in 1983 when Radio Carlisle became Radio Cumbria.

Donald's radio career took off again in the early 1990s when he began hosting his own Sunday afternoon shows at the Red Rose Radio in Preston in which he re-introduced his character of Gladys May. It was at this time that Donald appeared in his first

Donald (second from right) playing Luther Billis in a Carlisle Light Operatic Society production of South Pacific.

professional pantomime, *Little Red Riding Hood* at the Blackburn King George Hall. After leaving Red Rose Radio he was hired as Gladys the Cook by Carlisle's CFM Radio to guest Simon Grundy's afternoon show, which ran until 1998.

In December 1998 Donald starred in a Carlisle production of the pantomime *Dick Whittington*, just one of the many pantomimes he has appeared in.

In 1999 he joined BBC Radio Cumbria with his present day Sunday afternoon show *Donald at Lunchtime* in which he reviews the newspapers, plays favourite songs and chats informally to guests.

Donald has gained his greatest pleasure over the last three years whilst performing in David McNeil's pantomime productions at the Sands Centre, in front of a home crowd. He has also written his autobiography *Over the Garden Wall*.

Andrew Seivewright

Andrew Seivewright, became master of the music at Carlisle Cathedral in 1960 and was founder of the Abbey Singers. He read classics during his first year at King's College, Cambridge, later turning to music which he continued to study with Francis Jackson at York Minster.

As a conductor, Andrew Seivewright has worked with many types of choirs. He has considerable expe-

rience of broadcasting, both as a conductor and accompanist, and he has also been involved in the writing and production of music programmes for television.

In 1962 a small group of twelve amateur singers came together to sing *a cappela* music under the direction of Andrew Seivewright. Rehearsals took place within the Cathedral Close, known as 'The Abbey', hence the name of the choir.

By the time the photograph below was taken in April 1971, the Abbey Singers had grown to over 50 members. The soloist was Clifford Hughes who was a very versatile singer, educated at Dulwich College and then a choral scholar at King's College, before becoming a professional singer.

THE END OF THE YEAR COMPLETES A
SUCCESSFUL SEASON FOR THE

ABBEY SINGERS

Conductor: ANDREW SEIVEWRIGHT.

Engegements have included Concerts in Carlisle, Windermere, and Edinburgh and Broadcasts on Radio 4, I.T.V.
and B.B.C.

THE NEW SEASON BEGINS ON JANUARY 7th, WHEN
THERE WILL BE SOME VACANCIES, PARTICULARLY
FOR TENORS.
Apply to: 6 THE ABBEY, CARLISLE.

*An advert for an Abbey Singers performance, from the
Carlisle Journal, 1970.*

The choir was noted for its purity of tone, its accu-
racy and its musical interpretation of the works performed. They normally performed unaccompanied
choral music, with instrumental solos or ensembles
used to add variety in full length programmes.

The Abbey Singers have become well known
throughout England and Scotland, partly due to their
television appearances and radio broadcasts. They
have travelled to Europe and America to perform.

Bill Stephenson

Bill Stephenson left school in 1915 aged twelve.
Unable to take up a grammar school place he had won
due to lack of money as he came from a large family,
he took a job as a lather boy with Mr McGeary's hair-
dressers in Portland Square.

Mr McGeary was a keen amateur musician and
encouraged Bill to take up music. Bill saved up and
bought himself a cello and then a bass and became proficient in both. When Mr McGeary retired in the
1930s, Bill took a job in the Co-operative barbers shop
in Botchergate.

Bill joined the RAF in 1939 and was posted to
Reykjavik in Iceland, where he became a barber for
British RAF and American Air Force men. During the
war years he played in the RAF Band and the RAF
Bomber Command Band. At the end of the war he
returned to his position in Carlisle, eventually becoming manager of the Co-op ladies hairdressing salon.

The Tom Foster Band in the mid-1930s at the Queen's Hall, Viaduct. Bill is at the back and to the left.

Bill's musical achievements included playing for the Tom Foster Dance Band, the Mayfair Dance Band and the Alf Adamson Border Square Dance Band. In the latter band he was in the line up which made their TV debut in September 1955 at the National Radio Show, Earls Court. His family were extremely proud of him and not yet having their own television, went along to watch the programme at an aunt's house.

Bill also played in Her Majesty's Theatre Orchestra, accompanied shows by the Carlisle Choral and Musical Society and played music to accompany silent films at the Botchergate Picture House.

Bill with his hairdressing girls, from left, Margaret Armstrong, Doreen Robinson, Jennifer Kay, Norma Johnstone and Joan Schreiner in the mid-1960s.

Bill retired in 1969 and died, aged 77, in 1980, leaving his wife Mabel and two daughters, Irene and Elizabeth, or Liz, as she prefers to be known. Liz said that her father's nickname was 'Our Willie'.

Elizabeth Stewart

Elizabeth Stewart was born into a musical family. Her father, Jimmy Stewart, played the cornet for the St Stephen's Band from an early age, having been encouraged by his father, who was also a cornet player with the band. Jimmy played with the band into the 1960s, having taken time out only during

Elizabeth Stewart at the height of her career.

the First World War when he saw active service and again during World War Two, when he joined the fire service. Elizabeth's godfather was John Sullivan, manager of Her Majesty's Theatre; and her elder brother went on to become part-time assistant manager at Her Majesty's for a time. Monday night was theatre night for young Liz. She loved the sound of the big bands and recalls at an early age looking forward to going along with her father to Sunday morning band practises at the Market Hall.

The first time she and Donald Scott, her cousin sang together was when she was aged around eight. They took part in a talent contest at the Lonsdale Cinema.

Liz said, 'I can remember going to the audition with Donald. We were just a couple of kids, and scared stiff. I had sung with my school choir and given solo performances. Donald and I had played duets on the piano together in music festivals, but this was the first time we had sung in public. As we walked down the side of the cinema towards the stage door, we heard a baritone voice ringing out it sounded marvellous to us. We really didn't think we stood a chance.' However little Liz and Donald surprised everyone, including themselves, by coming out top in the competition.

Below, Elizabeth with the Two Bobbies, from left, Bobby Graham, Jimmy Norman on drums, Liz Stewart and Rob Dorrance.

Above, Elizabeth's father Jimmy Stewart, left, with Cyril Lowes and Tony Armstrong, of the St Stephen's Band.

Liz with Tequila Brass.

'We won £7.50 between us, and it seemed like a fortune to us, after that we got quite a few engagements locally.'

From the age of sixteen to twenty Liz was coached in her singing by the celebrated soprano Ena Mitchell. Liz enjoyed singing a numberr of parts with various amateur society shows in Carlisle and she and Donald had a very good song and comedy act which took them all over the north of England in their spare time. By day Liz worked as a hairdresser and Donald an interior decorator, (see Donald Scott).

In 1960 Liz married Alan Graham and moved to Gretna where she ran her own hairdressing salon. Around this time she was approached by Bobby Laing and asked to sing with the Jack Walker Trio at Dumfries, followed by another Scottish band, the Two Bobbies, which lasted until 1971 at which time she returned to Carlisle. Liz now ran a hairdressing salon on Castle Street, where in 1972 one of her clients was Mrs Dave Batey who asked Liz if she would be a stand in with the Dave Batey Trio as his regular singer had let him down. Liz did just that, performing at the Talk of the Border Club, much to the dismay of her parents. However the 'standing in' went on for weeks and she became exhausted, working her salon 9am to 6pm then at the club until 2am - she had to give it up.

In 1973 she was approached by Cliff Attwood (now leader of the Cliff Elland Band) to join his band, Tequila Brass. This position lasted until the 1980s.

Her last public performance was in 1985 when she guested on Donald Scott's show at the Stanwix Arts Theatre, Brampton Road. Liz does not sing these days, preferring people to remember her when she was at her best.

Billy Stewart

Billy Stewart ran Cumbrian Spotlights, a war time concert party based in Carlisle. Billy is synonymous with the firm of J P Dias Ltd, which was situated in Botchergate, where he was music teacher for over thirty years. He had an excellent reputation and 'anybody who was anybody' went to him to be tutored in their guitar playing. He also played in the Billy Stewart Band which performed at local venues.

The firm was originally founded in 1888 by James Patrick Dias. At first it was a pawnbroker's shop, buying and re-selling musical instruments and clothing. After the Second World War the pawn broking business became non-existent and the outfitter and music shop came into being. The ground floor was devoted to clothes and the top floor to musical instruments.

Because of increased demand for organs during the 1960s more space was required, so in 1968 the business branched into the building alongside the shop to accommodate Hammond Organs. The top floor was given over to Billy Stewart's music lessons.

Over the years the musical side of the business supplied instruments to many groups in Cumbria and parts of Scotland, from ukulele banjos during the George Formby era to guitars in the pop era. By 1968 it was estimated that the firm had sold around 10,000 guitars. They also had orders from abroad, sending piano accordions to the Persian Gulf and clarinets behind the Iron Curtain.

In 1963 when the boys of Harraby Secondary

The Billy Stewart Band, 1948, performing at the Palace Theatre, Botchergate. The boy on the right is Ritchie Jefferson who joined the Maurice Petry Trio.

153

Billy Stewart's guitar class, November 1963

School manufactured their own guitars in their wood work classes Billy Stewart became their tutor. The guitars were made out of African mahogany under the guidance of Mr Cyril Armstrong. At the time Billy said, 'The interest among the youngsters is terrific. They come for lessons in their spare time and many are shaping up very well. The guitars are excellent, sturdy with good tone and easy to handle. Production is going at full speed to get instruments ready for the do-it-yourself guitar enthusiasts' first public appearance before proud parents.' Teachers were interested too, and would get together for lunchtime jam sessions.

Bernie Summers

Bernie Holmes, better known to all as Bernie Summers is 60-years old and began his musical career more than 50 years ago, back when skiffle was popular. Since those days Bernie has entertained crowds and continues to do so.

As a youngster he took piano lessons but was more interested in skiffle being heavily influenced by the 'King of Skiffle', Lonnie Donnigan.

Bernie said, 'It was around 1954, just before I came out of the army that a fellow gave me his unwanted ukulele. I began listening to George Formby and taught myself to play it, for my own enjoyment at first. My very first public appearance came around 1956/57 when I went along to Her Majesty's Theatre to audition for 'Pick of the Town'. The manager, John Sullivan, asked me to return a week later with a length of string attached to my ukulele to hang it round my neck. From that audition I got to perform my George Formby impressions in two shows a day and the Saturday matinee. I was then asked to join the Terry Degnan Skiffle Group, who were also performing at Her Majesty's at that time.'

Bernie has a photograph collection, including one of the Terry Degan Skiffle Group on stage at Her Majesty's during an early country show extravaganza, long before the days when line dancing became popular in Britain.

He continued, 'When Terry Degnan left the group,

we became the Four Dollars. Other personnel changes occurred; drummer John Greerson left, he was replaced by Brian Rogerson for a while then Gordon Hind took over.'

Skiffle went out of fashion and the Four Dollars, namely, Johnny Mack, lead guitar, John Tickell, bass guitar, Gordon Hind, drums and Bernie Summers on guitar and vocals, turned themselves into a first class

Above, the Four Dollars at a Butlins talent competition, from left, Johnny Mack, John Tickell, Bernie Summers and John Greerson.

Below, the Four Dollars in 1963, from left, Johnny Mack, Bernie Summers, Adele Martin, Gordon Hind and John Tickell.

rock group with a difference. The difference being that as well as playing all the latest songs they put a touch of the 'Formby' and the 'Donnigan' into their act plus perhaps a few jokes about topical happenings. In 1961 this act took the Four Dollars into the grand Cameo final of the People National Talent Contest, held at the Metropole, Blackpool with a first prize of £1000. At the time John Tickell told the *Carlisle Journal*, 'Our act is definitely original. We are the oldest established rock group in Carlisle and easily the most travelled. We have played as far away as Inverness, and get regular bookings in West Cumberland and Durham.'

Incidentally Durham was the place the boys liked best. Bernie remembers returning from Durham one

155

Bernie Summers and his son Keith who have been performing as a duo for 20 years.

The VIPs

The VIPs were a soul/blues group whose members were Jim Henshaw, Mike Harrison, Greg 'Alf' Ridley, Frank Kenyon and Walter Johnston. After becoming fully professional in 1964 they quickly made three regional TV appearances, one on a top rated STV programme, *One Night Stand*, which was a very successful show. They also made two highly successful appearances at Liverpool's famous Cavern.

The group's manager was Mr Rodney Warr. They were rated by many as the north's top R & B group. The VIPs first made a disc around June 1964 but unfortunately it was never released. In the autumn of 1964 the group toured with Manfred Mann, whose recording of *Do Wah Diddy Diddy* had toppled the Beatles from their number one spot. The tour included Edinburgh, Birkenhead, Brighton and Newcastle. The VIPs also played at all the local venues, playing to audiences of around 1000 at a packed out Market Hall for Duncan McKinnon's Border Dances.

Their first single was released on 20 November 1964 - *Don't Keep Shouting at Me*, backed by *She's so Good* was issued on the RCA Victor Label. Both numbers were written by the leader of the group Jim Henshaw, who also saw his song *Blue Feeling*, recorded by the Animals, in the American charts having sold

night, 'We were travelling back form a gig. I remember the weather was atrocious. We were stuck in snow drifts over Stainmore and in the van stuck behind us was Jim Henshaw and the VIPs. We were prepared with our calor gas heater but the VIPs, who had no such luxury, were begging us to let them get into our van to warm up. We were having a laugh with them and not letting them in.'

In 1963 the Four Dollar line up was joined by Adele Martin. Adele sang with a vivacity that captured audiences, with her ballad style voice she was equally good at singing beat numbers and romantic songs.

Bernie said, 'The Four Dollars were together for around ten years then, when Johnny Mack left, a suitable replacement was hard to find. It was then that I decided to go solo. I paid £15 in a second hand shop for my auto harp, fitted it with electrical pick-ups which played through amplifiers and gave a great sound.'

'I signed up with the Newcastle based Beverly Agency, who sent me abroad to Sicily to do a gig. Locally I played around the pubs for seven years before being joined by my son, Keith. 20 years later we are still going strong.'

The VIPs' first visit to the Cavern in August 1964.

around 250,000 copies. Jim wrote other songs which were recorded by the Nashville Teens and songs which featured in American beach party movies.

In 1965 the VIPs popularity grew with a new 'bad boy' image when two of the band and their road manager Albert Heaton, appeared in court charged with trying to steal 24 railway detonators. Jim said, 'We had only gone in to make ourselves a cup of tea using the railway men's can and stove.'

After the release of their single *In A Dream*, in autumn 1965, they headed off to London, with Albert Heaton at the wheel of their blue Commer van, which was lined inside with carpet samples. The VIPs rehearsed at the Marquee Studios in London and went on to tour in France, Germany and the UK.

Recalling life as a VIP, Jim Henshaw said, 'In the beginning accommodation ranged from a shared cellar, somewhere in Berwick Street, to a cosy bed in anybody's flat. In a bid to make ends meet we modelled clothes for top designer Cecil Gee, appearing in teenagers' magazines. However we started to get quite a good following. We were the first group to have the

Above, the VIPs, from left, Frank Kenyon, Mike Harrison, Greg Ridley, Walter Johnston and Jimmy Henshaw, photograph courtesy of Norman Kenyon

Below, June 1965 and the VIPs were making a record for RCA, from top left clockwise, Jimmy Henshaw, Mick Harrison, Frank Kenyon, Alf Ridley and Walter Johnston.

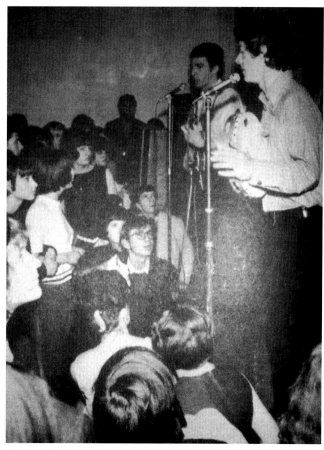

Above, the VIPs playing at Harraby Community Centre

Right, the contract to play at the Playboy Club.

residency at London's Playboy Club.'

The VIPs had been managed solely by Rodney Warr and CES Promotions until 1966 when the firm of CES signed with Mike Jefferies, manager of the Animals. With this agreement more bookings came in mostly from London's top rhythm and blues clubs. Working in the clubs they got to know two members of the Animals, vocalist Eric Burden and bassist Chas Chandler. Eric Burden said to the lads that their new disc *Wintertime* released in January 1966 would surely become a number one hit.

The VIPs played a major part in shaping music history, backing American guitar legend Jimmi Hendrix at his first ever British gig at the prestigious Scotch of St James Club in London. Jim recalls, 'Jimmi Hendrix played for about 15 to 20 minutes with us and got a standing ovation. Hendrix manager, Chas Chandler asked us to drop Mike Harrison and become backing group to Hendrix. We turned this offer down twice as we weren't about to drop Mike, for someone who at the time was a virtual unknown. Besides that we were all Carlisle lads and good mates too.'

The VIPs travelled to Hamburg where they began to visit the Star Club, where their whole sound and image really did take over where the Beatles had left off. Jim said, 'The Star Club was the top venue for rock 'n roll

bands, everybody played there - the Rolling Stones, Beatles, Jimmi Hendrix, Jerry Lee Lewis, Bill Hayley and many more. I think the crowning glory of my career came in 1970 when the Star Club was demolished and a black marble plaque was placed where the entrance had been. On this plaque were all the big names mentioned and also included up there with the greatest were the VIPs.'

The first adjustment to the line up happened in 1966 when, disillusioned by the life they were leading and homesick, drummer Walter Johnston left the group, to be replaced by Mike Kellie.

The new unrehearsed line up took the ferry from Dover to Dunkirk and drove to Paris where they appeared on a UNICEF variety show. Here they rubbed shoulders with the likes of Marlon Brando and Elizabeth Taylor. On their return to France some weeks later they found themselves with a number 2 hit record.

The VIPs were earmarked for the very top by critics and record companies alike. Their records received rave reviews, sold well and the band were the talk of the clubs throughout the country. However a string of mistakes meant they never quite made it to the top. They turned down the chance to record *All Day and All of the Night*, the song which shot unknown British act the Kinks into the limelight. Jim said, 'With hindsight, yes there could have been some wrong decisions

West End Promotions Ltd

DIRECTORS: C. H. PEERS, C. F. G. BLACKWELL

11, ARGYLL STREET, LONDON W.1   TELEPHONE: REGENT 8716

This Agency is not responsible for any non-fulfilment of Contracts by Proprietors, Managers or Artistes but every reasonable safeguard is assured.

Messrs ....

An Agreement made the ......27th...... day of ......JULY...... 19 66 between

......PLAYBOY CLUB...... (hereinafter called "the Management")

of the one part, and ......V.I.P's..... :

(hereinafter called the "Artiste") of the other part. Witnesseth that the Management hereby engages the Artiste and the Artiste accepts an engagement to appear/present as:
......KNOWN......

(or in his usual entertainment) at the Theatre/Club/Ballroom and from the dates for the periods and salaries stated in the Schedule hereto:

SCHEDULE

The Artiste agrees to appear at ......ONE...... performances at a
All equipment to be set up and ready for use by

salary of £ ...30... : ..... : .....   Arrival Time ......6.00 p...

......ONE...... Day(s) at ...PLAYBOY CLUB, LONDON...... commencing ......11TH SEPTEMBER...... 19 66

......Day(s) at ......   commencing ...... 19 ......

......Day(s) at ......   commencing ...... 19 ......

SPECIAL CLAUSES:

1. It is agreed that ......THE ARTISTE...... shall appear in person throughout the entire performance of his act.

2. and microphone equipment.

3. The Artiste/Band shall not, without the written consent of the management appear within ......miles of the towns mentioned herein for ......weeks prior to and during this engagement, and for ......afterwards.

4. Performance times to be decided by the management but it is agreed that ......THE ARTISTE...... shall appear in ...(TBN)... (8.00 p.m. – 2.00 a.m. ½ hour on – ½ hour off)

5. Transportation to be provided by ......THE ARTISTE......

6. Photos and Bill matter to be sent to this office not later than twenty-one days before opening.

7. All financial settlement to take place with ...WEST END PROMOTIONS LTD... within ...SEVEN DAYS... of completion of engagement

The Commission accruing from this engagement shall be equally divisible between Les Farrel representing Playboy Club and West End Promotion

I/We the undersigned acknowledge that I/we have read the above special clauses and agree that they will be adhered to in detail.

taken, but at the time they were the right ones for us with our style of music and also the right decisions for the song writers.'

Jim Henshaw recalls another opportunity missed, 'The Artistes and Repertoire man for Island Records, Guy Stevens, introduced a young DJ to us, who had written some songs and it was suggested that we put music to them. One of his songs was *A Whiter Shade of Pale*. We decided we couldn't do anything with it in our style so it got passed on to an unknown outfit called the Paramounts, which included a classical organist who proceeded to put music to the song. Soon after they changed their name to Procul Harum and the rest is history.

'It later transpired that solicitors had got Walter Johnston to sign a document saying he had nothing to do with *A Whiter Shade of Pale* as he had done the drumming for the demo disc. A sessions drummer was brought in for the recording and told to copy Walter's drum style. I know Walter's drum technique and every time I hear it I can't help thinking that either the sessions drummer was very good at mimicking Walter or it is in fact Walter's drums on the record.'

Despite never quite reaching the top there were many highs in a career which won them contracts with a string of Britain's top record labels, including Island, CBS and RCA. By late December 1966 they were heading back to Carlisle and whilst coming over Shap Jim announced his departure from the group. His departure was soon followed by Frank Kenyon and so the VIPs split up with members going their separate ways.

Art, the four man group which includes two former VIPs, in December 1967.

After returning to Carlisle when the VIPs had split up, Frank Kenyon went on to form Junkyard Angel and a new group Art was formed by former VIPs Michael Kellie, Luthor Grosvenor, Mike Harrison and Greg Ridley. Art was a London based group which almost broke into the top with their debut and, as it turned out, their only single *What's the Sound*.

The band 'went dark' for a while and then were back on the scene in January 1968 with an extra member and a new name, Spooky Tooth. They consisted of ex-VIPs Mike Harrison and Greg (Alf) Ridley, bass guitarist; Luther Grosvenor, lead guitarist and Michael Kellie the Birmingham-born drummer who had taken over when Walter Johnston had left the VIPs. The new member was 21 year old Gary Wright, on piano, an American who brought a group to Europe from America and stayed to join Spooky Tooth. Gary was the composer of Spooky Tooth's debut disc.

In May 1968 after a performance at the Cosmo manager Les Leighton, who was also manager of the 101 Club, was so delighted with the boys sound that he decided to pay them a tribute. Les named the beat weekends at the 101 the 'Spooky Tooth Segments'.

Following the break up of the VIPs, Jim Henshaw joined Tambourine a Carlisle based group, playing with Mike Gillen on rhythm guitar, Ernie Green on bass guitar and Ian Carruthers on drums. Tambourine split on friendly terms in October 1969 with everyone planning to go their separate ways. Jim went on to play with Bandstand, Cottage and then, in the 70s, with Captain Flint.

In October 1977 Jim founded Carlisle's first recording studio in the unlikely surroundings of an old mill on Junction Street. He moved £4000 worth of sound equipment, including an eight track recording machine, much of it home-made, into the premises.

By 1979 Jim realised this humble eight track in Junction Street wasn't going to produce the next number one. So, whilst in the process of moving house, Jim bought a former girls' school, Wykeham House on the corner of Lismore Place with Warwick Road.

Spooky Tooth whose LP was acclaimed as the best from the Island label in 1969. The band had a great deal of success in America.

He teamed up with night club boss Tom Foster. The two went halves on all the equipment for a new studio, with Jim's electronic wizardry helping to cut the cost a little, resulting in Carlisle's first 16 track recording studio. Bands could use the facility for £10 an hour. Jim's next step was to advertise nationally and through local agent Andy Park began to invite visiting bands to record with him.

Walter Johnston who went on to play drums with the Les Taylor Combo and Lemongrass. Walter was asked to join Procul Harum after doing a demo disc with them for 'A Whiter Shade of Pale'. Walter turned down the offer and the group found another drummer.

Alf Ridley joined Humble Pie, playing with Peter Frampton and Steve Marriot, and is pictured here in 1971.

Below, Jim Henshaw outside the old Wykeham House School.

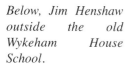

Rodney Warr

Rodney Warr lived at Summer Hill during the 1950s and was much in demand for his comedy and singing skills. His trademark costume was a dinner jacket and cummerbund. During the day he worked at Binns' store as an assistant buyer in the mens' department.

Rodney Warr with Rue and the Rockets

Below, Rodney as Frankie Vaughan

Rodney began entertaining at concert parties and charity shows when he was still a boy. When he left school he trained for professional theatre in his home town of Oxford. Life as a budding actor was a financial struggle and the profession was crowded so Rodney decided to leave and came to Carlisle in 1954.

He began doing his variety shows in and around the

city, many of which were devoted to raising funds for charity. He often performed at Her Majesty's Theatre and was an immediate success. In 1958 he began impersonating Frankie Vaughan and eventually got to meet him - Frankie gave his blessing to the act.

Rodney also managed groups such as the VIPs and Rue and the Rockets. He appeared on television in *The Top Town* series. His favourite entertainers were Ella Fitzgerald, Sammy Davis Jnr, Peggy Lee and Danny Kaye. He was also keen on sports such as football, cricket and tennis. In the late 1970s Rodney moved to Sheffield.

Above, a presentation was made to Rodney Warr by Dai Watkins on the occasion of his leaving Carlisle.

Top, Rodney Warr as Eamonn Andrews for a spoof 'This is Your Life' show.

Dennis Watt

Dennis Watt's earliest memories of playing guitar go back to a front room in Currock Road with a friend, Maurice Caullihole and two of his friends, a drummer and a lead guitarist. 'We would play instrumentals from the Shadows, such as *Apache* and *Gonzales* together with hits like *Saturday Night at the Duck Pond* and *El Commanchero*, indeed we called ourselves the Commancheros. We were later joined by Mike Baxter. I must have been about fifteen,' said Dennis.

The Voltaires playing at the County Ballroom, from top left clockwise, Dennis Watt, Ian Meldrum, Ray Parr, Terry Maxted and Rob Holliday.

He continued, 'In those days a gig would be playing at the local youth club, and like a lot of would be Hank Marvins, we would pay our two shillings and go to guitar teacher, Billy Stewart, at Dias' shop for our weekly lesson. Billy would take the sheet music and rewrite the bass, rhythm and lead parts for us. We would learn one tune per week.'

In the early 1960s Dennis left Maurice and his friends to join the Voltaires, namely Ian Meldrum on drums, Ray Parr on lead guitar, Robin 'Polly' Holliday on bass guitar, Terry Maxted as vocalist and Dennis Watt on rhythm guitar.

Dennis said, 'Our first booking was at the County and shortly afterwards we became the first group to play alongside the dance bands in the Cameo Ballroom. When we played our first number, mainly due to Polly's enormous 18 inch Wharfedale bass speaker, years of dust fell from the intricate ceiling.'

Other bookings were at the Silver Grill, the Crown and Mitre ballroom, the Gretna Hall, the Queen's Hall and at the Stomp Ins on Sunday nights at the Cosmo. More bookings followed, mainly in West Cumbria, after they joined up with Border Entertainments Agency, owned at the time by Mr Jenkins of Pioneer Foods and managed by Rodney Warr. Dennis recalls,

The Dolls at Whitehaven Civic Hall, 1965, from left, Paul McLachlan, Brian Dunk, Ian Meldrum, Rob Holliday and Ray Parr (front).

'The Voltaires became committed to rhythm and blues, we changed our name to the Dolls which at the time was VERY progressive.'

After the demise of the Dolls Dennis went on to become part of the country band, Silver Dollar for a time before joining another successful country band, Country Breeze. Later in the 1980s as part of the Odd Balls, along with Geoff Dickens, he played on stage at the first Great Fair held in Carlisle.

Dennis and his wife Fiona left Carlisle in the early 90s and headed for the warm sunshine of the island of Crete where they ran a bar for a while, before moving to Holland where they still live today.

CARLISLE AND DISTRICT YOUNG FARMERS

GRAND DANCE

in

THE COSMO

The Mayfayre Band and The Dolls

On FRIDAY, 18th SEPTEMBER,

from 8 p.m. to 1 a.m.

Tickets available at the Cosmo 5/- each

YOU HAVE BEEN ENTERTAINED BY:

John Abba
Rod Adams
Alf Adamson
Olly Alcock
Ian Alecock (Mel Adams)
Pat Allen
Johnny Alone
Alec Alves
Ronnie Archibald
Alan Armstrong
Eric Armstrong
Lance Armstrong
Pete Arnison
Jacky Atherton
Rhonda ?
Dick Atkinson
Gordon Atkinson
Jacky Atkinson
Jimmy Atkinson
Ronnie Atkinson
Cliff Attwood
Ken Attwood
Sandy Axon

Ian Barnes
Tommy Barnett
Chris Barton
Ted Barton
Dave Batey
Derek Batey
Gerald Batey
Pete Batey
Roy Batey
George Baxter
Mike Baxter
Tommy Baxter
Alison Bayne
Pam Bayne
Phil Bayne
Ray Begg
Arthur Belcher
Kenneth Belcher
Dave Bell
Stan Bell
Sam Bellingham
Geoff Betsworth
Jason Black
David Blackburn
Charlie Blake
Dennis Blamire
Cliff Bond
Boz Borrowdale

John Boss
Billy Bowman Snr.
Billy Bowman Jnr.
Florrie Bowman
John Bowman
Ken Bowman
Jazzer Boyle
Tennent Brow
Derek Brown
Phil Brown
Bonzo Burns
Malcolm Butcher
Malcolm Butterfield

Paul Caddick
Neil Caddle
Brian Cadonna
Henry Cadonna
Bill Cain
David Carrick.
Mostyn Carpentor
Ian Carruthers
Gwynne Challenger
Mike Charlton
Bernie Cheeseman
David Clapperton
Trish Clarke
Billy Collins
Brian Collins
George Collins
Charles Cook
Phil Cook
John Corson
John Coulthard
Brian Cowen
Mike Crosby
Roger Crosby
Arthur Curwen
Billy Currey

Ray Daly
Brian Davies
Terry Degnan
Geoff Dickens
Les Dock
Bill Douglass
Molly Douglass
Arthur Duckworth
Brian Duffell
Eric Duffell
Bob Duncan
Brian Duncan

Doreen Duncan
Ian Duncan
Brian Dunk

Billy Edmondson
Teddy Edmondson
Ben Eggleston
Cliff Eland
John Ellwood
Michael Ewbank

Don Farley
Steve Fearns
George Fehrenbach
Kenny Fell
Kathleen Ferrier
Bill Finlayson
Kenny Fitzpatrick
John Forster
Dave Foster
George Foster
Tom Foster
Peter Frampton
Eric Freeman

James Garner
Howard Gaughey
Peter Gausis
Tommy Giacopazzi
David Gibson
Mike Gillen
John Goldie
Bobby Goodger
Bill Gore
Arthur Graham
Chris Graham
Frances Graham
Janet Graham
Liz. Graham
Sinclair Graham
Thomas Graham
Ian Grant
Ernie Green
Ken Green
Jack Green
John Greerson
Bob Grice
Luther Grosvenor

Albert Halliday
Gordon Halliwell
Derek Hannah

Dorothy Harding
Mary Harding
Jim Harrison
Mike Harrison
Kenny Hartness
Norman Heeley-Creed
Gordon Henshaw
Jimmy Henshaw
Ian (Sherb) Herbert
John Hetherington
John Higgins
Jack Highman
Peter Hill
Tony Hill
Gordon Hind
Bob Hinkley
Peter Hoban
Norman Hodgson
Ronnie Hodgson
John Hogarth
Robin Holliday
John Hope
Ernie Horn
John Horrocks
Ivan Hunter
Jock Hymen

Bob Irving
Rita Irving
Ronnie Irving
Terry Irving
Joy Irving
Maurice Irwin
Kevin Iveson

Bobby Jackson
Joe Jackson
Billy James
Ivor James
Ritchie Jefferson
Richard Jennings
Stewert Jesset
Gerry Johnston
Gil Johnston
Dave Johnston
Jean Johnston
Walter Johnston
Tom Jones
Dick Jordon

Ian Kellet
Mike Kelly

Bob Kendal
Kenny Kendal
Tommy Kenedy
Dave Kent
Frank Kenyon
Stuart Kenyon
Ken Kirby

Tommy Laidlow
Gordon Lamb
Bobby Laing
Chas. Leask
Dave Lee
Les Leyton
Peter Lince
Arthur Ling
Dave Little
Graham Little
Stanley Little
Frank Logan
Joy Logan
Phil Logan
Tommy Lomas
Tony Lommi
Brian Lorimor
Bert Lowes
Cyril Lowes
Geoff Lowes
William Lowes
Harold Lowry
Rob Lowther
Ronnie Lowther
Graham Luck
Alan Lyall

Zeppo Mac
Johnny Mack
Dickie Macgrath
Steve Marriot
Neil Marshall
Adele Martin
Raymond Martin
Ronnie Martin
Malcolm Mason
Terry Maxted
Michael Maxwell
Peter McCaffery
Olly McCauley
Tex McEatin
Dave McCormiskey
Alan McCubbin
John McGaughlin
Phil McGenn
John McGuiness
Rob McHendry
Duncan McKenzie

John McKie
Michael McKie
Paul McLachlan
Stan McManus
David McRae
John McVicar
Keith McVicar
Ian Meldrum
Brian Melville
Laura Metcalfe
Dave Midgely
Howard Midgeley
Arnold Miller
Terry Mills
George (Mad) Mitchelhill
Dennis Mitchell
Ena Mitchell
Ian Mitchell
Andrew Monk
Syd Monk
Geoff Morris
Scot Morris
Stan Morrison
Barry Moses
Tom Moses
Harold Muir
Peter Murray
Robert Murray
Peter Myers

Harvey Naylor
Chris Nicholson
Fred Nicholson
Barry Nixon
Ted Nixon
Billy Noble
Gordon Norman

Brian Oliver
Jimmy Oliver
Ron Oosthuizen

Thelma Palmley (née Hope)
George Pape
Ray Parr
Ralph Pennington
Maurice Petry
John Porthouse
Al Potts
John Potts
Micky Potts
Euan Pringle
Raymond Purves

Ida Radcliffe
Roland Reid
Tony Renney
Alf Ridley
Harry Roberts
Ann Robertson
Caral Robinson
George Robinson
Brian Rogerson
Billy Rook
Harald Routledge
Billy Rowe
Bob Ruddick
Dave Ruddick
Dave Rutherford
George Rutherford

Boris Sanderson
Terry Savage
Donald Scot
Fred Scot
Dave Scotson
Andrew Seivewright
Alan Sessford
Brian Sewell
Mike Shannon
Ronnie Shaw
Howard Sims
Terry Sims
Billy Simpson
Red Skelton
Alec Slane
Alan Slater
Jimmy Slater
Rueben Slater
Chris Smith
Eric Smith
John 'Maitland' Smith
Sycamore Smith
Colin Spark
Alf Stephenson
Bill Stephenson
Billy Stewart
Jimmy Stewart
Liz Stewart
Ian Stockdale
Dave Storey
Ces Stubbs
Bernie Summers
Keith Summers
Ronnie Swarbrick
Jack Sykes

David Taylor
Roger Taylor
Tony Tears

Russ Thomlinson
Bill Thompson
Mal Thoreburn
The Thwaites Family
John Tickell
Derek Tolson
Rob. Towers

Herbert Vicar
Larry Vicars

Lindy Waddell (née Rum)
Ronnie Walker
Dai Walters
Tommy Walton
Laurence Wannop
Terry Ward
Rodney Warr
Dai Watkins
Annie Watson
Jimmy Watson
Pete Watson
Stan Watson
Dennis Watt
R. West
Dennis Westmorland
Goerge Whitehead
Mike Wilding
Harald Wilkinson
Keith Wilkinson
Jim Willis
Tim Wilson
Brian Witherington
Eric Wood
Colin Wright
Gary Wright
James Wyllie

CONCLUSION

I would like to pay tribute to the entertainers and musicians who worked so closely together during the mid-20th century.

Sadly a visit to Carlisle Cemetery, shows that some of those people are no longer with us though, even in death there are close links with Ronnie Atkinson's grave lying next to Cliff Eland's and, within just a few metres, are the ashes of Arthur 'Danny' Curwen. Frank Kenyon's grave is nearby, as is that of Ray Purves.

The sounds of the big band and the crooners of the 1950s have been laid to rest too. They were replaced by the new sound of pop, with small bands of musicians who could entertain large numbers of people at a fraction of the cost of a big band. Then live music of all kinds was threatened in the early 70s by the introduction of discos, such as Scamps, where one person could operate the music.

December 1973 and one of the first purpose built discos in the country opened in Carlisle.

Research for this book has produced a wealth of information and photographs, so much so, that not everything could be included. The book tries to cover as wide a spectrum as possible but sincere apologies to anyone who has been missed out or who finds their favourite musician not included. The authors have enjoyed this trip down memory land, the research and meeting the stars and hope that you, the reader, have enjoyed it too. In the words put to the music of a Russian folk song made famous by Mary Hopkin in September 1968 when it went to No 1 in the charts:

> *Those were the days my friends,*
> *We thought they'd never end,*
> *We'd sing and dance forever and a day.*

MORE BOOKS FROM HAYLOFT

Oil, Sand & Politics, Memoirs of a Middle East Doctor, Mercenary and Mountaineer, Dr Philip Horniblow (£25, ISBN 1 9045240 9 5)

The Maddison Line, Roy Maddison (£10, ISBN 1 9045240 6 0)

A Herdwick Country Cook Book, Hugh & Therese Southgate (Hardback, £19.95, ISBN 0 9540711 8 2) (Paperback, £14.95, ISBN 0 9540711 7 4)

The Long Day Done, Jeremy Rowan-Robinson (£9.50, ISBN 1 9045240 4 4)

From the High Pennines, Marmaduke Alderson (£10, ISBN 1 9045240 7 9)

Pashler's Lane, A Clare Childhood, Elizabeth Holdgate (£10, ISBN 0 9542072 0 3)

Odd Corners in Appleby, Gareth Hayes (£8.50, ISBN 1 9045240 0 1)

The Ghastlies, Trix Jones and Shane Surgey (£3.99, ISBN 1 9045240 4 4)

A Journey of Soles, Lands End to John O'Groats, Kathy Trimmer (£9.50, 1 9045240 5 2)

Changing the Face of Carlisle, The Life and Times of Percy Dalton, City Engineer and Surveyor, 1926-1949, Marie K. Dickens (£8, ISBN 0 9540711 9 0)

From Clogs and Wellies to Shiny Shoes, A Windermere Lad's Memories of South Lakeland, Miles R. M. Bolton (£12.50, ISBN 1 9045240 2 8)

A History of Kaber, Helen McDonald and Christine Dowson, (£8, ISBN 0 9540711 6 6)

The Gifkin Gofkins, Irene Brenan (£2.50, ISBN 1 9045240 1 X)

A Dream Come True, the Life and Times of a Lake District National Park Ranger, David Birkett (£5.50, ISBN 0 9540711 5 8)

Gone to Blazes, Life as a Cumbrian Fireman, David Stubbings (£9.95, ISBN 0 9540711 4 X)

Changing Times, The Millennium Story of Bolton, Barbara Cotton (£12.50, ISBN 0 9540711 3 1)

Better by Far a Cumberland Hussar, A History of the Westmorland and Cumberland Yeomanry, Colin Bardgett (Hardback, £26.95, ISBN 0 9540711 2 3) (Paperback, £16.95, ISBN 0 9540711 1 5)

Northern Warrior, the Story of Sir Andreas de Harcla, Adrian Rogan (£8.95, ISBN 0 9523282 8 3)

2041 - The Voyage South, Robert Swan (£8.95, 0 9523282 7 5)

Yows & Cows, A Bit of Westmorland Wit, Mike Sanderson (£7.95, ISBN 0 9523282 0 8)

Riding the Stang, Dawn Robertson (£9.99, ISBN 0 9523282 2 4)

North Country Tapestry, Sylvia Mary McCosh (£10, 0 9518690 0 0)

To Bid Them Farewell, A Foot & Mouth Diary Adam Day (£14.50, ISBN 1 90452 41 0 9)

Military Mountaineering, A History of Services Expeditions, 1945-2000, Retd. SAS Major Bronco Lane (Hardback, £25.95, ISBN 0 9523282 1 6) (Paperback, £17.95, ISBN 0 9523282 6 7)

Secrets and Legends of Old Westmorland, Peter Koronka and Dawn Robertson (Hardback, £17.95, ISBN 0 9523282 4 0) (Paperback, £11.95, ISBN 0 9523282 9 1)

The Irish Influence, Migrant Workers in Northern England, Harold Slight (£4.95, 0 9523282 5 9)

Soldiers and Sherpas, A Taste for Adventure, Brummie Stokes. (£19.95, 0 9541551 0 6)

Between Two Gardens, The Diary of two Border Gardens, Sylvia Mary McCosh (£5.95, 0 9008111 7 X)

A Riot of Thorn & Leaf, Dulcie Matthews (£7.95, ISBN 0 9540711 0 7)

Dacre Castle, A short history of the Castle and the Dacre Family, E. H. A. Stretton (£5.50, 0 9518690 1 9)

Little Ireland, Memories of a Cleator Childhood, Sean Close (£7.95, ISBN 0 9540673 0 4)

A Slip from Grace, More tales from Little Ireland, Sean Close (£9.99, ISBN 0 9540673 1 2)

Isaac's Tea Trail, Roger Morris (£2)

Antarctica Unveiled, Scott's First Expedition and the Quest for the Unknown Continent, David E. Yelverton (£25.99, 0 8708158 2 2)

You can order any of our books by writing to:
Hayloft Publishing Ltd,
South Stainmore, Kirkby Stephen,
Cumbria, CA17 4DJ, UK.
Please enclose a cheque plus £2 for UK postage and packing.
or telephone: +44 (0)17683) 42300
For more information see: www.hayloft.org.uk